CROCKPOT RECIPES BOOK

Most Delicious Rich and Savory Crockpot Chicken Recipes

(Easy Crock Pot Chicken Recipes and Tips for Perfect Slow Cooker Meals)

Bill Lopez

Published by Alex Howard

© Bill Lopez

All Rights Reserved

Crockpot Recipes Book: Most Delicious Rich and Savory Crockpot Chicken Recipes (Easy Crock Pot Chicken Recipes and Tips for Perfect Slow Cooker Meals)

ISBN 978-1-990169-92-2

All rights reserved. No part of this guide may be reproduced in any form without permission in writing from the publisher except in the case of brief quotations embodied in critical articles or reviews.

Legal & Disclaimer

The information contained in this book is not designed to replace or take the place of any form of medicine or professional medical advice. The information in this book has been provided for educational and entertainment purposes only.

The information contained in this book has been compiled from sources deemed reliable, and it is accurate to the best of the Author's knowledge; however, the Author cannot guarantee its accuracy and validity and cannot be held liable for any errors or omissions. Changes are periodically made to this book. You must consult your doctor or get professional medical advice before using any of the suggested remedies, techniques, or information in this book.

Table of contents

Part 1 1
Delicious Slow Cooker Recipes 2
1) Beef Chili 3
2) Chicken Verde 5
3) Turkey Breast and Herb-Cornbread Stuffing 7
4) King Ranch Chicken 9
5) Butternut Squash-parsnip Soup 11
6) Chicken with 40 Cloves of Garlic 13
7) Chocolate-Walnut Bread Pudding 15
8) Cheesy Spinach Crab Dip 17
9) Triple-Berry Cobbler 19
10) Lamb Tagine 21
11) Pumpkin Spice Latte 23
12) Pork and Slaw Sandwiches 25
13) Shrimp and Sausage Gumbo 27
14) Balsamic Collard Greens 29
15) Mexajita Chicken 31
16) Apple Butter 33
17) Mulled Wine 35
18) Chicken Cacciatore with Spaghetti 37
19) Spicy Fajita Soup 39

20) Caribbean-Style Pork 41

21) Cranberry Punch 43

22) Maple Hazelnut Oatmeal 45

23) Thai Red Curry Beef 47

24) Roasted Garlic White Bean Dip 49

25) Salsa Cheesecake 51

26) Honey Orange Carrots 53

27) Spiced Beef with Sweet Potatoes 55

28) Berry Lemonade Tea 57

29) Meatloaf 59

30) Pumpkin Spice White Hot Chocolate 61

Slow-Simmered Meat Sauce with Pasta (beef) 63

Sauerbraten (beef) 64

Beef And Beans 66

Beef And Bratwurst 67

Beef And Gravy 68

Beef Barley Soup 69

Beef Stew 70

Casserole 71

Breakfast quinoa 72

Cinnamon rolls 74

Chicken and potatoes and carrots 76

Collard greens with bacon and balsamic vinegar 77

Honey Ribs and Rice (Pork) 79

Chinese Pork Roast 80

Curried Lentil-Tomato Soup (Pork) 81

Part 2 84

Introduction 85

2. Size and Servings: 92

3. Time: 92

4. Liquids: 93

1. Convenience: 93

2. Ready-to-go Meals: 94

3. Tender Meat: 94

4. Versatility: 94

Chicken Recipes 97

Comforting Chicken Stew: 97

Crock Pot Balsamic Boneless Chicken Thighs: 99

Chicken Tikka Masala: 101

Flavorful Chicken and Gravy: 103

Lemon Grass and Coconut Chicken: 104

Indian Chicken Curry: 106

Crock Pot Chicken Lo Mein: 108

Roasted Chicken with Lemon & Parsley Butter: 111

Tender Cilantro Lime Chicken: 112

Keto Jerk Chicken: 114

Sweet and Tangy Chicken: 115

Slow Cooker Moscow Chicken: 117

Greek Chicken 119

Delicious Butter Chicken: 120

Easy-Breezy Fajita Chicken: 123

Beef Recipes 125

Soul Warming Beef Stew: 125

Crockpot – Low Carb Short Beef Ribs: 127

Braised Corned beef Brisket: 129

Chili Lime Shredded Beef: 130

Exotic Middle Eastern Beef: 132

Richly Taste Beef Chili: 133

Mexican Crockpot Beef Roast: 135

Italian Beef for Sandwiches: 137

Tasty Pulled Beef: 139

Pepper Beef Tongue Stew: 141

Sweet & Tangy Beef Shoulder: 143

Ronaldo's Beef Carnitas: 145

Smokey Beef Brisket: 146

Indian Beef Stew 148

Divine Beef Shanks 150

Lamb Recipes 152

Keto Lamb Barbacoa: 152

- Greek Lamb Roast: 154
- Tasty Lamb Shoulders: 155
- Island Lamb Stew: 157
- Basic Lamb Stew: 158
- Thyme Lamb Chops: 160
- Garlic Lamb Roast: 161
- Garlic Herbed Lamb Chops: 163
- Tamil Attukal Paya Dish: 164
- Lamb Shanks with Tomatoes: 166
- Delicious Balsamic Lamb Chops: 168
- Pot Roast Soup: 169
- Lamb Curry: 171
- Crockpot Ropa Vieja: 173
- Ground Lamb Casserole: 175
- Pork Recipes 177
- Fabulous pork Casserole: 177
- Chili Pulled Pork Tacos: 179
- Root Beer Pulled Pork: 181
- Cuban Pulled Pork: 182
- Pork Stew with Oyster Mushrooms: 184
- Beamless Pork Chili: 186
- Pork Roast with Sugarless Chimichurri Sauce: 188
- CONCLUSION 190

Part 1

Delicious Slow Cooker Recipes

1) Beef Chili

Tender and spicy beef chunks tossed in herbs, vegetables and peppers infuse sizzling flavors in each bite. This can be served with noodles or any dip sauce of your choice. In this recipe we will serve it with spiced sour cream.

Yield: 4

Total Prep Time: 6 hours

List of Ingredients:

- Beef chuck roast, 1, cubed
- Red pepper flakes, ½ tsp.
- Garlic, 1 tbsp., minced
- Kosher salt
- Jalapeno peppers, 1, chopped
- Canola oil, 2 tbsp.

- Beef broth, 1 cup
- Chili powder. 1 tsp.
- Black pepper
- Cinnamon, ½ tsp.
- Tomato, 1 can, chopped
- Yellow onions, 2, chopped
- For spiced sour cream:
- Sour cream, ½ cup
- Scallions, 2
- Lime juice, 1 tsp.
- Hot sauce, 1 tsp.
- Chili powder, 1 tsp.

Procedure:

Heat oil in a wok and add beef.

Season it with salt and pepper. Cook for 15-20 minutes. Transfer beef chunks to a paper towel and remove excess oil from the wok.

Add beef broth to the slow cooker.

Now add beef and season the mixture with red pepper flakes, jalapeno, cinnamon, chili powder, onions and garlic.

Stir well. Add tomatoes and cover the lid. Let it cook for 6 hours on low temperature.

For spiced sour cream, combine all the ingredients well in a small bowl and serve with beef.

2) Chicken Verde

Planning a fancy dinner? How about adding Chicken Verde to the menu? It is a southwestern entrée which is prepared with roasted poblano and tossed in jalapeno peppers, onions and tomatillos. This recipe makes enough servings for 6 people.

Yield: 6

Total Prep Time: 3 ½ hours

List of Ingredients:

- Bone-in chicken breasts, 6, halved
- Poblano chilies, 5
- Ground black pepper, ½ tsp.

- Sour cream, 1/3 cup
- Garlic, 5 cloves, minced
- Onion, 2 cups, chopped
- Cilantro, ¼ cup
- Sugar, 1 tbsp.
- Jalapeno peppers, 4
- Green chilies, 1 can, drained and chopped
- Canola oil, 1 tbsp.
- Ground cumin, 1 ½ tsp.
- Tomatillos, 5 ½ cups, chopped

Procedure:

Preheat a boiler and char jalapeno and poblano for 10 minutes by putting them on a foil-lined baking tray. When the skin is nicely charred, cover the peppers in a plastic bag and close tightly. Leave for 15 minutes.

Now peel them and remove their seeds and membranes. Chop them finely.

In a large bowl, mix chopped peppers with onions, tomatillos, garlic, green chilies and sugar. Toss well.

Coat chicken breasts with cumin and black pepper. Heat oil in a skillet and cook chicken over medium-high flame. When the chicken turns light brown put it in a 6-quart slow cooker and add the pepper mixture. Cover the lid and cook for 3 ½ hours on low temperature.

When the chicken is tender, separate it from the sauce and boil the sauce in a saucepan. Let it simmer for 25 minutes.

Garnish chicken with cilantro and sour cream. Serve with sauce.

3) Turkey Breast and Herb-Cornbread Stuffing

This recipe makes a delicious Thanksgiving meal. Herbs and cornbread infuse together to bring out an exotic combination of flavors that will be loved by everyone on the table.

Yield: 8

Total Prep Time: 4 hours

List of Ingredients:

- Bone-in and skin-in turkey breast, 1
- Onion, ½ cup, chopped
- Pepper, ¼ tsp.

- Eggs, 2, beaten
- Butter, ¼ cup
- Celery, ½ cup, chopped
- Buttermilk cornbread mix, 1 package
- Herb-season stuffing mix, 1 ½ cups
- Parsley, ¼ cup, chopped
- Salt, 1 tsp.
- Chicken broth, 1 can
- Poultry seasoning, 1 ½ tsp.

Procedure:

Make cornbread mixture according to the directions given on the back of the package. When cornbread mixture cools down completely, crumble it.

Season turkey with salt and pepper.

Melt butter in a skillet and cook turnkey breast with skin side downwards. Cook until it turns nice brown. Now remove meat from the skillet and sauté onions, parsley and celery in the same skillet.

In a large bowl combine broth with cornbread, onion mixture, eggs and stuffing mix.

Grease a 6-quart slow cooker with a little butter and pour the mixture along with turkey. Cook for 4 hours on low temperature.

Serve after 15 minutes of removing from the cooker.

4) King Ranch Chicken

This is an extremely rich and cheesy recipe that makes amazing casserole. The ingredients like cream of chicken soup and cream of mushroom soup make it undeniably filling and tempting at the same time.

Yield: 6

Total Prep Time: 4 hours

List of Ingredients:

- Cooked chicken, 4 cups, shredded
- Fajita-size corn tortillas, 12
- Cream of mushroom soup, 1 can
- Garlic, 1 clove, minced
- Onion, 1, chopped
- Cream of chicken soup, 1 can
- Chili powder, 1 tsp.

- Green bell pepper, 1, chopped
- Diced tomatoes and green chilies, 1 can
- Cheddar cheese, 2 cups, shredded

Procedure:

Mix chicken with bell peppers, onions, cream of soups, garlic, tomatoes and chili powder.

Break tortillas into 1'inch pieces.

Grease a 6-quart slow cooker and spread 1/3 layer of tortillas. Then make another layer of 1/3 chicken and 2/3 cup of cheese. Make 2 similar layers. Cover the lid and cook for 3.5 hours on low temperature.

Uncover after the stated time, if the edges are golden brown let it cook for another 30 minutes uncovered.

5) Butternut Squash-parsnip Soup

This recipe makes an extremely delicious soup for a cold winter afternoon. With the perfect spices and balanced savory taste, this soup is simple to make. The cream gives the soup a nice creamy texture and taste.

Yield: 8

Total Prep Time: 6 hours

List of Ingredients:
- Parsnip, 2 cups, chopped
- Paprika, 1/8 tsp.
- Water, 3 cups
- Whipping creams, 2 tbsp.
- Light sour cream, ½ cup
- Sweet onion, 2 cups, chopped
- Ground cumin, 1/8 tsp.

- Salt, ¼ tsp.
- Ground black pepper, 1 tsp.
- Fresh chives, 8 tsp., chopped
- Chicken broth, 2 cups
- Granny smith apple, 1 ½ cup, peeled and chopped
- Butternut squash, 3 packages, thawed

Procedure:

In a 5-quart slow cooker, pour water and chicken broth. Add onions, apple, parsnip, squash, salt and pepper.

Cook for 6 hours on low temperature.

After 6 hours, blend the mixture in the batches of 2 in a blender. Let the steam escape before blending by removing the center part of blender lid. Make a smooth mixture.

Pour the soup in a large serving bowl.

Add cumin, paprika and whipping cream. Stir once.

Garnish with chives and sour cream.

6) Chicken with 40 Cloves of Garlic

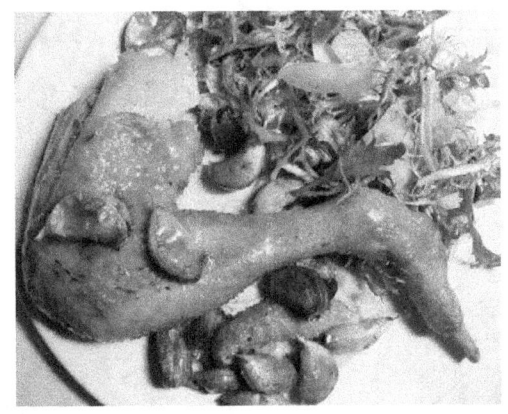

This recipe is of North African descent. It is seasoned with herbs that infuse the flavors of chicken when mixed with apricot to make a glazing sauce. This recipe is perfect for a grand dinner and of course, very unique.

Yield: 4

Total Prep Time: 8 hours

List of Ingredients:

- Whole chicken, 1
- Garlic cloves, 40, peeled
- Thyme leaves, 1 tbsp., chopped
- Ground black pepper, ½ tsp.
- Dried apricots, 1 cup

- Vegetable cooking spray
- All-purpose flour, 1 tbsp.
- Unsalted chicken stock, ½ cup
- Rosemary spring, 1
- Butter, 4 tbsp., melted
- Kosher salt
- Thyme springs, 8
- Dry white wine, ¼ cup

For garnishing:
- Thyme
- Rosemary springs

Procedure:

Cover the bottom of the cooker with aluminum foil. Slightly coat foil with vegetable cooking spray and add 3 tbsp. butter, apricot, thyme, garlic and rosemary springs.

Now put chicken and season with salt and pepper.

Pour wine and chicken stock. Cover the lid and cook for 8 hours on low temperature.

When chicken is tender, transfer it to the serving platter. Add garlic on the sides.

With the help of cheesecloth squeeze the liquid from the cooker in a bowl and boil 1 cup of it in a saucepan.

Stir flour and mix continuously for until the sauce becomes thick.

Add chopped thyme and serve with the chicken.

7) Chocolate-Walnut Bread Pudding

Here is another delicious dessert recipe to end the cookbook with a sweet goodbye. Made with chocolate, walnuts and cinnamon bread, this pudding makes an indulging chocolate cake with fudgy texture and coffee cream sauce swirling all over.

Yield: 8

Total Prep Time: 2 hours

List of Ingredients:
- Semisweet chocolate pieces, ¾ cup

- Walnuts, ½ cup, chopped
- Presweetened cocoa powder, ¾ cup
- Coffee cream sauce
- Milk, 3 cups
- Eggs, 3, beaten
- Cinnamon swirl bread, 5 cups

Procedure:

Grease a 4-quart slow cooker with nonstick cooking spray.

Heat milk in a saucepan. Do not boil. Remove from heat and add chocolate and cocoa. Without stirring keep aside for 5 minutes. Now whisk the mixture and form a smooth texture.

In a bowl add eggs with chocolate mixture. Add walnuts and bread cubes. Pour this mixture in the greased cooker and cover the lid.

Cook for 2 hours or until the toothpick inserted inside comes out clean. Cook on low temperature.

Remove from the cooker and let it cool for around 30 minutes.

Dish out in serving bowls and top it up with coffee cream sauce.

8) Cheesy Spinach Crab Dip

This recipe makes a perfect delectable appetizer with little preparation time. The ingredients include lemon, vinegar and cream that give a nice tangy and creamy hint of flavor all at once. This makes for a great party starter!

Yield: 20

Total Prep Time: 2 hours

List of Ingredients:

- Lump crab meat, 1 ½ cups, shells removed
- Canola mayonnaise, ½ cup
- Lemon rind, 1 tsp., grated
- Ground red pepper, ½ tsp.
- Fat-free milk, ½ cup

- Sherry vinegar, 1 tbsp.
- Fat-free sour cream, 1 carton
- Garlic, 2 cloves, minced
- Onion, ½ cup, chopped
- Cheddar cheese, 1 cup
- Frozen spinach, 1 package, thawed and chopped
- Cream cheese, 1 tub
- Parmesan cheese, ¾ cup

Procedure:

Combine all the ingredients except for lemon rind in a 3-quart slow cooker.

Mix all the contents well and let it cook for 2 hours on low temperature.

Pour in a dipping bowl and sprinkle lemon rind.

Serve with whole-grain crackers or pita chips.

9) Triple-Berry Cobbler

This recipe is a delicious blend of blackberries, blueberries and raspberries. Each bowl is loaded with sweetness and an extraordinary taste that serves as a perfect end to any meal.

Yield: 6

Total Prep Time: 1 hour

List of Ingredients:

- Blackberries, 2 cups
- Raspberries, 2 cups
- Blueberries, 2 cups
- Milk, 2 tbsp.
- Water, 1 cup
- All-purpose flour, 1 cup
- Sugar, 1 cup
- Baking powder, 1 tsp.

- Vegetable oil, 3 tbsp.
- Quick cooking tapioca, 3 tbsp.
- Ground nutmeg, ¼ tsp.
- Salt, ¼ tsp.
- Eggs, 2, beaten
- Sugar, ¾ cup
- Ground cinnamon, ¼ tsp.
- Vanilla ice cream

Procedure:

In a large bowl combine flour with cinnamon, ¾ sugar, nutmeg, salt and baking powder.

In another bowl whisk eggs with oil and milk. Add this to the flour mixture and combine well.

In a saucepan toss sugar and tapioca over the berries. Add water and boil.

Add the berries mixture to a 4-quart slow cooker and stir the egg-flour batter. Cover the lid and cook for 1 hour or till the toothpick inserted in the center comes out clean. Cook on high temperature.

Remove from the cooker and let it stand for an hour to set,

Spoon into serving bowls and top it with vanilla ice cream.

10) Lamb Tagine

Lamb tagine is a flavorsome supper like meal with balanced sweetness and is savory also. It has saffron that gives it a hint of yellowish color and a nice flavor. The tenderness of lamb gives a meaty and authentic taste in every bite.

Yield: 6

Total Prep Time: 7 hours

List of Ingredients:

- Boneless leg of lamb, 2 pounds, cut into small cubes
- Saffron threads, ¼ tsp., crushed
- White onion, 2 cups, chopped
- Cooked couscous, 3 cups, hot
- Pumpkin pie spice, 1 tsp.

- Chicken broth, ½ cup
- Honey, 2 tbsp.
- Ground cumin, 1 tsp.
- Orange, 1 navel
- Ground red pepper, ¼ tsp.
- Salt, ½ tsp.
- All-purpose flour, 2 tbsp.
- Plums, 1 cup, dried and pitted
- Almonds, 2 tbsp., toasted and peeled

Procedure:

Squeeze about ¼ cup orange juice and grate the rind about 2 tsp.

Stir flour in the orange juice and whip to form a smooth texture. Add rind and mix well.

Over medium-high flame, sauté lamb in a large pan for 10 minutes. Add chicken broth and let it simmer for a few minutes.

Now add orange-flour mixture and combine the contents well.

Add onions, cumin, red pepper, pumpkin pie spice, salt and saffron and combine all the ingredients well.

Transfer the lamb mixture to a 3-quart slow cooker and cook for 6 hours on low temperature.

When the lamb meat is tender, add honey and dried plums and cook for an additional 1 hour.

Dish out in a serving platter and garnish with toasted almonds. Serve with couscous.

11) Pumpkin Spice Latte

Fall is never too far around the corner which means colorful pumpkins everywhere. Pumpkins are the season's delight and what is better than making a delicious latte with a hint of pumpkin spice? Absolute Pleasure!

Serving: 10

Total Prep Time: 2 hours

List of Ingredients:
- Strong brewed coffee, 5 cups

- Heavy whipping cream, ½ cup
- Sugar, 1/3 cup
- 2% milk, 4 cups
- Vanilla, 1 tsp.
- Canned pumpkin, ¼ cup
- Pumpkin pie spice, 1 tsp.
- Additional whipped cream for topping

Procedure:

Put all the ingredients in a slow cooker.

Cover the lid and cook for 2 hours on high temperature.

After every hour stir once.

Pour the mixture in serving mugs and swirl whipped cream atop.

12) Pork and Slaw Sandwiches

This is a classic pork sandwich. The recipe makes plentiful servings with minimal preparation time. If you use packaged coleslaw you can save your time. Hot sauce and barbeque sauce give a fiery flavor to the pork and vinegar adds a strong flavorful touch.

Yield: 15

Total Prep Time: 8 hours

List of Ingredients:
- Boneless pork loin roast, 3 pound
- Hot sauce, 1 ½ tbsp.
- Salt, 1/8 tsp.
- Barbeque sauce, 1 ¾ cups
- Sugar, ¼ tsp.
- Canola mayonnaise, ¼ cup
- Water, 1 cup

- Brown sugar, 2 tbsp.
- White vinegar, 1 tbsp.
- Ground black pepper, ½ tsp.
- Coleslaw, 2 ½ cups
- Hamburgers buns, 15

Procedure:

Cook pork with water in a 3 quart slow cooker for 7 hours on low temperature.

Drain the liquid from pork and put it back in the slow cooker and shred using 2 forks.

Add black pepper, hot sauce, barbeque sauce and brown sugar. Cover the lid and cook for an additional 1 hour on low temperature.

In a mixing bowl, combine coleslaw with the remaining ingredients. Toss well.

To prepare sandwiches, put 1/3 pork and 2 tbsp. coleslaw on the bottom of the bun and put the upper top of the bun over it.

13) Shrimp and Sausage Gumbo

This recipe is a traditional Louisiana classic made with shrimps and sausages spiced with peppers and seasoning. It is a hearty meal suitable for any occasion. In no time your platter will be empty and your guests will be craving for more.

Yield: 6

Total Prep Time: 6 hours

List of Ingredients:

- Andouille sausage, 1 pound, sliced
- Shrimps, 3 pounds, peeled and deveined
- All-purpose flour, ½ cup
- Parsley, ¼ cup, chopped
- Green bell pepper, 1, chopped
- Chicken broth, 4 cups

- Green onions, 1 bunch, chopped
- Dried thyme, ½ tsp.
- Bay leaves, 3
- Diced tomatoes, 1 can
- Creole seasoning, 2 tsp.
- Garlic, 4 cloves, minced
- Onion, 1, chopped
- Celery ribs, 2, chopped
- Garnishing: chopped green onions

Procedure:

Preheat oven to 400F. Dust flour over a skillet and bake for 15 minutes.

Cook sausages in a Dutch oven until browned. Transfer to paper towels and let it stand for 5 minutes.

Now add sausages, tomatoes, thyme, onion, celery, garlic, bay leaves, bell peppers and creole seasoning to a 5-quart slow cooker.

Combine flour and broth together in a bowl and form a smooth mixture. Add it to the cooker and cover the lid. Cook for 6 hours on high temperature.

Later add shrimps, parsley and green onions. Cover again and cook for an additional 30 minutes.

14) Balsamic Collard Greens

Green is not only healthy, but it's also pleasing to the eye. Collard greens are healthy green leaves from the family of cabbage and broccoli. When combined with bacon and other spices, they make an amazing meal which can be served with mashed potatoes.

Yield: 5

Total Prep Time: 4 hours

List of Ingredients:

- Bacon slices, 3
- Honey, 1 tbsp.
- Chicken broth, 1 can
- Onion, 1 cup, chopped
- Bay leaf, 1
- Balsamic vinegar, 3 tbsp.

- Collard greens, 1 package, chopped
- Garlic, 2 cloves, minced
- Salt, ¼ tsp.

Procedure:

Roast bacon slices in a large skillet. Roast until they become crispy on medium flame.

Remove from the skillet and sauté onions in the same skillet. Add collard green and cook for 5 minutes.

Crumble bacon slices and keep aside.

When the collard greens are cooked put them in a slow cooker and add minced garlic, salt and chicken broth. Cook for 4 hours on low temperature.

For serving, mix vinegar with honey and add to collard greens along with bacon.

15) Mexajita Chicken

Mexajita chicken cooked in slow cooker is a flavorful meal that is super simple to cook with boneless chicken, pinto beans and spicy fajita seasoning. It tastes super delicious with sautéed bell peppers and onions seasoned with fajita seasoning.

Yield: 4

Total Prep Time: 4 hours

List of Ingredients:
- Boneless skinless chicken breast, 4
- Fajita seasoning, 1 tbsp.
- Canola oil, 3 tbsp.
- Pinto beans, 2 cans, un-drained
- Salt
- Mexican diced tomatoes, 2 cans
- Pepper

Procedure:

Season chicken with salt and pepper.

Heat oil in a skillet and cook chicken breasts. For a more beautiful texture and flavor sprinkle some salt and pepper while the chicken is frying.

When the meat changes into a nice golden brown color transfer it to a 5-quart slow cooker.

Add beans and canned tomatoes. Season with fajita mix and cover the lid.

Cook for 4 hours on low temperature.

16) Apple Butter

Surprised by the name? Yes! The slow cooker is not only restricted to making meaty meals but it can also make other types of food in it. This is a unique apple butter spread recipe that can be served alongside pork chops or can be spread over a muffin.

Yield: 4 cups

Total Prep Time: 10 hours

List of Ingredients:
- Apple, 10, sliced into chunks and peeled
- Brown sugar, 1 cup
- Ground cinnamon, 1 tbsp.
- Ground mace, 1/8 tsp.
- Apple cider, ¼ cup
- Ground cloves, ¼ tsp.

- Honey, ½ cup

Procedure:

Put all the ingredients in a slow cooker and cook for at 10 hours on low temperature.

Using a sieve squeeze liquid from the apple mixture. Put sieve over a bowl and put half of the apple mixture in it. With the help of a spoon press the mixture. Remove pulp and put the remaining mixture in the sieve and repeat the step.

Put the liquid back in slow cooker and cook for an additional 1.5 hours without covering the lid. Let a thick paste like consistency be formed.

Serve with muffins or pork chops.

Store remaining in the jar and keep in refrigerator.

17) Mulled Wine

This wine recipe tastes like Christmas holidays! The blend of spices and orange juice enhances the flavor of wine, leaving a subtle and rustic taste on your tongue. By adding brown sugar you cut down the stringent flavor of the wine and can enjoy the flavor for as long as you like.

Yield: 3

Total Prep Time: 3 hours

List of Ingredients:
- Red wine bottle, 1
- Orange, 1
- Cinnamon sticks, 2
- Brown sugar, ¼ cup
- Whiskey, 2 oz.

- Whole cloves, 3
- Triple sec, 1 oz.
- All spice berries, 5

Procedure:

Squeeze half of the orange juice and thinly slice the remaining half. Keep aside.

In a 4-quart slow cooker add red wine, orange juice, triple sec, cinnamon sticks, all spice berries and cloves. Also add orange slices.

Cover the lid and cook for 3 hours on low temperature.

Before serving the wine add brown sugar and whisky.

Remove whole spices using the slotted spoon.

Pour into wine glasses and enjoy.

18) Chicken Cacciatore with Spaghetti

Spaghetti is a common favorite loved by everyone. They make a great snack with room for plenty of variations. This recipe makes a hearty and delicious sauce, when combined with spaghetti makes a filling meal.

Yield: 6

Total Prep Time: 8 hours and 30 minutes

List of Ingredients:

- Bone-in chicken leg quarters, 2
- Bone-in chicken breast, 2
- Garlic, 6 cloves, minced
- Butter, 2 tbsp.
- Yellow onions, 1, chopped
- Spaghetti, 1 package
- Dried crushed red pepper, 1 tsp.

- Red bell pepper, 2, chopped
- Tomato paste, 3 tbsp.
- Parmesan cheese, ¼ cup, grated
- Green bell pepper, 2 chopped
- Ground black pepper, 1 tsp.
- White wine, ½ cup
- Kalamata olives, 1 ½ cup, pitted and halved
- Cremini mushrooms, 1 can. Sliced
- Fire-roasted diced tomatoes, 1 can
- Kosher salt, 1 tbsp.
- For garnishing, basil cheese and parsley

Procedure:

In a large bowl coat chicken with tomato paste and wine. Now season with salt, red pepper and black pepper. Add garlic, onions, bells peppers and mushrooms. Add drained roasted tomatoes and combine everything well.

Put the chicken and vegetable mixture in a 6-quart slow cooker and cook for 8 hours on low temperature.

After 8 hours, remove chicken and cook the sauce on high temperature for 30 minutes.

Cook pasta in water with a pinch of salt. Drain pasta through cold running water and set aside.

Shred chicken and combine it with sauce and spaghetti. Add olives, butter and grated cheese.

Sprinkle basil and fresh parsley along with some parmesan cheese.

19) Spicy Fajita Soup

Spicy fajita soup is a delicious soup recipe prepared with tomatoes, corn and onions in an aromatic seasoned chicken broth. Cheese and adobo sauce brings out a tempting creamy and spicy flavor. This is perfect for a cold winter evening.

Yield: 4

Total Prep Time: 5 hours

List of Ingredients:

- Chicken broth, 1-quart
- Yellow onions, 2, chopped

- Scallions, 2, chopped
- Chile powder, 2 tbsp.
- Tomatoes, 1 can, diced
- Monterey jack cheese, 1 cup, shredded
- Garlic, 1 tbsp., chopped
- Green peppers, 2, cored and seeded, cut into strips
- Canola oil, 2 cups
- Frozen corn, ½ cup
- Kosher salt
- Black pepper
- Chipotle pepper in adobo sauce, 1, chopped
- Corn tortillas, 12, cut into eighths

Procedure:

Add onions, broth, chipotle, corn, 1 tbsp. chili powder, garlic, peppers and tomatoes in a slow cooker and cook for 5 hours in low temperature.

In a large wok, heat oil and fry corn tortillas until they become crisp. Transfer to a paper towel and season with salt and 1 tbsp. chili powder and toss well.

Now preheat a boiler and in meantime pour soup in a bowl and add cheese. Place the bowl on a pan and broil until the cheese turns brown.

Top the soup with scallions and serve with corn tortillas.

20) Caribbean-Style Pork

Bell peppers are the key ingredient of this recipe. They add a nice hint of sweetness and crispiness to the pork. They also make the dish look colorful and appetizing. For a filling meal serve it with cooked rice.

Yield: 6

Total Prep Time: 6 hours

List of Ingredients:

- Pork loin roast, 1, boneless and center cut
- Garlic, 2 cloves minced
- Hoisin sauce, 2 tbsp.

- Cumin seeds, 1 tsp., crushed
- Lime juice, 1 tbsp.
- Salt, ½ tsp.
- Red bell peppers, 2 cups, sliced
- Crushed red peppers, ½ tsp.
- Soy sauce, 1 tbsp.
- Creamy peanut butter, 2 tbsp.
- Olive oil, 1 tsp.
- Green onions. 6, cut into small pieces
- Cooking spray
- Green onions, 2 tbsp., diagonally cut
- Cooked basmati rice, 4 ½ cups

Procedure:

Cut pork meat into 1'inch pieces. Grease a large skillet and sauté meat on medium flame until they turn brown.

Now grease a 4-quart slow cooker and fill it with roasted pork, green onions and bell peppers. Mix everything well.

In an another bowl, stir hoisin sauce, garlic, salt, peanut butter, soy sauce, cumin seeds, crushed red peppers and lime juice. Combine all the contents thoroughly.

Add this mixture to the slow cooker and cook everything on high temperature for 1 hour. Later, turn the temperature to low and cook for additional 5 hours.

Sprinkle 2 tbsp. green onions and serve with rice.

21) Cranberry Punch

Cranberry punch is a blend of cranberries with cinnamon and pineapple juice. Each glass is filled with a refreshing flavor, perfect for any occasion. This is a unique drink you can serve to your guests, whether you invite them to a lunch party or a dinner soiree.

Yield: 3

Total Prep Time: 10 hours

List of Ingredients:

- Cranberry juice, 4 cups
- Cinnamon stick, 1
- Packed brown sugar, ½ cup
- Unsweetened pineapple juice, 4 cups
- Whole cloves, 1 tsp.
- Water, 1 cup

Procedure:

In cheesecloth tie together cinnamon and cloves.

Stir all the ingredients in a slow cooker.

Cover the lid and cook for 10 hours on low temperature.

Pour in serving glasses and dip a lemon piece in each glass.

22) Maple Hazelnut Oatmeal

Oatmeal is a truly healthy ingredient. Not only does it serve as a filing breakfast but it can also be eaten as a midday snack. Maple syrup and cinnamon add a unique flavor of sweetness and a hint of bitterness topped with hazelnuts. This recipe is ultimate happiness served in a small bowl.

Yield: 4

Total Prep Time: 7 hours

List of Ingredients:
- Steel-cut oats, 1 cup, uncooked
- Fat-free milk, 1 ½ cups
- Butter, 1 ½ tbsp.
- Maple syrup, ¼ cup
- Brown sugar, 2 tbsp.
- Salt, ¼ tsp.

- Water, 1 ½ cups
- Ground cinnamon, ¼ tsp.
- Gala apples, 2, peeled and cubed
- Hazelnut, 2 tbsp., chopped
- Cooking spray

Procedure:

In a wok combine water and milk together and bring to a boil while stirring repeatedly.

Grease a 3-quart slow cooker with cooking spray and pour the boiled milk in it. Add apples oats, cinnamon, salt, brown sugar, and butter. Combine all the contents well. Cover the lid and cook for 7 hours on low temperature.

Serve with maple syrup and hazelnuts on top.

23) Thai Red Curry Beef

The key ingredient of this recipe is a jalapeno seed that adds a delicate fiery touch to the flavor of beef and other herbs. This makes for a filling meal when served with rice.

Yield: 8

Total Prep Time: 6 hours

List of Ingredients:

- Lean beef stew meat, 2 pounds
- Beef broth, ¾ cup
- Jalapeno pepper, 1, sliced
- Garlic, 4 cloves, minced
- Red curry paste, 3 tbsp.
- Light coconut milk, 1 can
- Salt, 1/8 tsp.

- Fish sauce, 2 tbsp.
- Basil leaves, ½ cup
- Dark brown sugar, 1 tbsp.
- Onions, 2 cups, chopped
- Baby spinach leaves, 2 cups
- Lime juice, 2 tbsp.
- Jasmine rice, 4 cups

Procedure:

Cook beef in a large skillet until it turns brown in color. Transfer beef to a 4-quart slow cooker and season with salt.

In the same skillet sauté onions and garlic until translucent. Put broth, sugar, jalapeno, red curry paste, lime juice, fish sauce and coconut milk in the slow cooker. Add sautéed onion and garlic. Cover the lid and cook for 6 hours on low temperature.

After 6 hours, add spinach and cook for an additional 20 minutes.

Garnish basil leaves over beef and serve with hot rice.

24) Roasted Garlic White Bean Dip

White beans are high in fiber and potassium. This recipe makes a hearty dip with roasted garlic combined with ricotta to bless it with a smooth consistency. Kalamata olives and rosemary blend together and give it a light bitter flavor. They can be served with crackers.

Yield: 15

Total Prep Time: 2 hours

List of Ingredients:

- Cannellini beans, 2 can, washed and drained
- Kalamata olives, ¼ cup, pitted and roughly chopped
- Ricotta cheese, 1 cup
- Rosemary, 1 tsp., chopped
- Ground black pepper, ¼ tsp.
- Olive oil, ¼ cup
- Lemon rind, ½ tsp., grated

- Parmesan cheese, ¾ cup, grated
- Water, 1/3 cup
- Garlic, 6 cloves, chopped

For garnishing:

- Black pepper and rosemary

Procedure:

Sauté garlic over low flame in a small pan.

Blend beans and water together and add ricotta cheese, sautéed garlic, rosemary, parmesan cheese and black pepper. Form a smooth mixture.

Pour this mixture in a 3-quart slow cooker. Cover the lid and cook for 2 hours on low temperature.

Pour in the serving bowl and add lemon rind and olives.

Sprinkle black pepper and rosemary atop.

25) Salsa Cheesecake

This unique cheesecake will make your guests envy your cooking skills and the deliciousness you served at the table. This recipe requires a little effort but the results are worth it in the end.

Yield: 20

Total Prep Time: 2 hours

List of Ingredients:

- Dry breadcrumbs, 1 tbsp.
- Yellow bell pepper, 3 tbsp., chopped
- All-purpose flour, 1 tbsp.
- Salsa, ½ cup
- Hot water, 4 cups
- Egg, 1
- Egg white, 1

- Chili powder, 2 tsp.
- Green onions, 3 tbsp., chopped
- Green chilies, 1 can, chopped
- Ground cumin, 1 tsp.
- Cooking spray
- Tomato, ¼ cup, seeded and chopped
- Light cream cheese with chives and onions, 1 tub, softened
- Pre-shredded reduced fat 4-cheese Mexican blend cheese, 1/2 cup
- Cilantro, ¼ cup, chopped
- Cream cheese, 1 tub, softened

Procedure:

Grease a 7 inch pan with cooking spray and coat the bottom with breadcrumbs. Cover the bottom and edges with foil

Whisk cream cheese with a mixer and form a smooth consistency. Now add flour, cumin, salsa, chili powder and green chilies and beat again to mix well.

Stir egg white and egg to the mixture and beat again. Lastly add Mexican blend cheese and mix.

Transfer the mixture to the prepared pan.

Put a ramekin upside down in a 5quart slow cooker. Put the prepared pan over the ramekin and add hot water in the cooker. Make sure you do not spill water over the mixture. Cover the top with paper towels and put on the lid.

Cook for 1 hour and 45 minutes on high temperature.

When the cake is set, discard paper towels and without removing the pan from cooker run a knife around the edges of the cake. Remove the cake from cooker and let it cool for 30 minutes.

Remove from the pan and let it stand to chill for 24 hours.

Before serving sprinkle with cilantro, bell peppers, tomato and green onions.

26) Honey Orange Carrots

Carrots are a treat to enjoy during winter. Although we have frozen carrots all year long but the taste of fresh and juicy carrots is undeniable. This recipe makes an awesome side dish glazed with butter and honey.

Yield: 13

Total Prep Time: 8 hours

List of Ingredients:

- Carrots, 3 pound, diagonally cut into pieces
- Salt, ½ tsp.
- Orange rind, ½ tsp., grated
- Honey, ½ cup
- Butter, 2 tbsp., cut into pieces
- Water, 2 tbsp.

Procedure:

In a 4-quart slow cooker, add carrots, honey and water. Season with salt.

Add butter and cover the lid. Cook for 8 hours in low temperature.

Sprinkle orange rind on top while serving.

27) Spiced Beef with Sweet Potatoes

This recipe is praiseworthy for any festive occasion. The mighty bowl of beef tossed with butternut squash and sweet potatoes will be praised by everyone. If you want to be the prominent chef of any party, try this recipe and see how people will love it.

Yield: 8

Total Prep Time: 7 hours

List of Ingredients:

- Boneless chuck roast, 1, cut into small cubes
- All-purpose flour, 3 tbsp.
- Dried thyme, 1 tsp.
- Salt, 1 ½ tsp.
- Beef broth, 1 container

- Ground pepper, 1 tsp.
- Smoked paprika, 1 tsp.
- Tomato paste, 1 can
- Olive oil, 2 tbsp.
- Celery, 2 ribs, chopped
- Small sweet potatoes, 2 pound, peeled and cut into cubes
- Ancho chile powder, 2 tsp.
- Butternut squash, 2 cups, cubed
- Garlic, 4 cloves, minced
- Sweet onions, 2, sliced
- Frozen corn, 2 cups

Procedure:

Combine tomato paste with beef broth and form a thick paste.

Coat beef chunks with flour and season with salt and pepper.

Preheat oil in a skillet. Add beef and cook until they turn brown in color. Now transfer beef to a 6-quart slow cooker.

Add tomato and broth paste. Also add sweet potatoes, thyme, paprika, corn, squash, celery, ancho chili powder, onions, garlic and smoked paprika.

Cover the lid and cook for 7 hours on high temperature.

28) Berry Lemonade Tea

A refreshing blend of tea and lemonade with a hint of fruity touch makes this exotic tea perfect for every season. Serve it chilled or hot according to your mood. This recipe makes 12 servings perfect for any occasion.

Yield: 12

Total Prep Time: 3 hours

List of Ingredients:

- Tea bags, 12
- Honey, 1/3 cup
- Lemons, 2, sliced

- Water, 8 cups
- Frozen mixed berries, 1 package
- Natural lemonade, 5 cups, chilled

Procedure:

Remove tea from its bag. Put it in a 5-quart slow cooker with berries, honey, lemonade and water. Cover the lid and cook for 3 hours on low temperature.

Top each serving with lemon slices. Serve cold or warm.

29) Meatloaf

This recipe makes 6 servings of a hearty and meaty meal. The savory meatloaf will turn out to be a crowd-pleaser. With only a handful of ingredients, you will be able to treat your guests with the most delicious meatloaf ever.

Yield: 6

Total Prep Time: 6 hours

List of Ingredients:

- Ground round, 2 pounds
- Yellow mustard, 1 tsp.
- Egg, 1
- Ketchup, 1 cup
- Dry onion soup mix, 1 envelope
- Light brown sugar, 1 tbsp.

- Cheddar cheese, 1 cup, shredded
- Worcestershire sauce, 1 tbsp.
- Dry breadcrumbs, ¾ cup

Procedure:

In a large bowl coat meat with breadcrumbs, onion soup mix, beaten egg, Worcestershire sauce and cheddar cheese.

Add ¼ cup water and ½ cup ketchup. Combine everything well and shape it into a loaf.

Cover the bottom of a 4-quart slow cooker with aluminum foil and slightly coat it with oil.

Put the loaf in the slow cooker and add mustard, ketchup and brown sugar. Spread it evenly over the loaf.

Cover the lid and cook for 6 hours on low temperature or until meat is thoroughly cooked.

Serve with quinoa or vegetables.

30) Pumpkin Spice White Hot Chocolate

An upsize cup of hot chocolate is a winter favorite. Loaded with cinnamon, nutmeg, whipped cream and pumpkin, the richness of this recipe makes a perfect combination of a sweet and spicy treat.

Yield: 4 cups

Total Prep Time: 2 hours

List of Ingredients:

- Pumpkin puree, ¼ cup
- Whole milk, 4 cups
- Cinnamon sticks, 4
- Ground ginger, 1/8 tsp.
- White chocolate chip, 1 cup
- Nutmeg, 1 tsp., grated
- Vanilla extracts, 2 tsp.

For serving:
- Nutmeg, whipped cream
- Cinnamon sticks

Procedure:

Add all the ingredients in a 2-quart slow cooker and cook on low temperature for 2 hours.

Stir frequently in the first hour and occasionally in the second.

Pour white chocolate in 4 serving cups, swirl whipped cream and sprinkle a pinch of nutmeg and add cinnamon sticks.

Slow-Simmered Meat Sauce with Pasta (beef)

Ingredients:

1 tablespoon olive oil

2 cups chopped onion

1 cup chopped carrot

6 garlic cloves, minced

2 (4-ounce) links hot Italian sausage, casing removed

1 pound ground sirloin

1/2 cup kalamata olives, pitted and sliced

1/4 cup no-salt-added tomato paste

1 1/2 teaspoons sugar

1 teaspoon kosher salt

1/2 teaspoon crushed red pepper

1 (28-ounce) can no-salt-added crushed tomatoes, undrained

1 cup no-salt-added tomato sauce

1 tablespoon chopped fresh oregano

16 ounces uncooked mafaldine pasta

1/2 cup torn fresh basil

3 ounces shaved fresh Parmigiano-Reggiano cheese

Directions:

1. Heat a large skillet over medium-high heat. Add oil to pan.

2. Swirl to coat. Add onion and carrot to pan. Sauté 4 minutes, stirring occasionally. Add garlic. Sauté 1 minute, stirring constantly.

3. Place vegetables mixture in a 6-quart crock pot. Add sausage and beef to skillet. Sauté 6 minutes or until browned.

4. Stirring to crumble. Remove beef mixture from skillet using a slotted spoon.

5. Place beef mixture on a double layer of paper towels, drain.

6. Add beef mixture to crock pot. Stir olives and next 6 ingredients: (through tomato sauce) into crock pot. Cook on LOW 8 hours. Stir in oregano.

7. Prepare pasta according to package Directions. Omitting salt and fat. Serve sauce with hot cooked pasta; top with basil and cheese.

Sauerbraten (beef)

Ingredients:

1 cup water

2 tablespoons sugar

3/4 cup white vinegar

1 1/2 teaspoons salt

6 black peppercorns

5 whole cloves

3 bay leaves

1 lemon, sliced

1 (3-pound) rump roast, trimmed

1 1/2 cups sliced onion (1 large)

15 gingersnaps, crumbled

(Chopped fresh parsley, optional)

Directions:

1. Place first 8 ingredients: in a large heavy-duty zip-top plastic bag; seal bag. Turn bag to blend marinade. Place roast and onion in bag; seal bag, turning to coat. Marinate in refrigerator 24 hours, turning bag occasionally.

2. Removed roast from marinade, reserving marinade. Place roast in a 5-quart electric crock pot. Strain reserve marinade through a sieve into a bowl, reserving 1 1/2 cups; discard remaining liquid and solids. Pour 1 1/2 cups strained marinade over roast. Cover and cook on LOW for 5 hours or until roast is tender.

3. Remove roast from crock pot; cover and keep warm. Add gingersnap crumbs to liquid in crock pot. Cover and cook on LOW for 8 minutes or until sauce thickens; stir with a whisk until smooth. Serve sauce with roast. Garnish with parsley, if desired.

Beef And Beans

Ingredients:

1 1/2 pounds of stewing beef

1 tablespoon prepared mustard

1 tablespoon taco seasoning

1/2 teaspoon salt

1/4 teaspoon pepper

2 garlic cloves diced

16 oz. diced tomatoes, undrained

1 medium chopped onion

1 Can kidney beans rinsed and drained

1 can chili beans

(1 Can black beans, optional)

Directions:

1. Mix mustard, taco seasonings, salt, pepper and garlic in a large bowl. Add beef and toss to coat!

2. Put the beef in the crock pot while adding the rest of the ingredients.

3. Cover and cook for 6-8 hours on LOW heat.

4. Serve along with hot rice.

Beef And Bratwurst

Ingredients:

1 pound beef

1 bratwurst

3 potatoes

1/2 small red onion

3 medium protabello mushrooms, quartered

1 packet of beef au ju, powder

5 cups water

Directions:

1. First, put water and au ju powder in the crock pot and stir to mix.

2. Put the remaining Ingredients in the pot and cook on LOW heat till the meat is cooked, and high for 20-30 minutes before serving.

3. Serve with French bread

Beef And Gravy

Ingredients:

2-3 pounds roast cut into bite sized pieces

1 packet of Lipton's Onion soup mix

2 rang of cream of mushroom soup

Directions:

1. Place pieces of the roast in a crock pot.

2. Sprinkle the packet of onion soup on the meat and cover with cream of mushroom soup.

3. Let it cook for 8 hours and stir midway through cooking.

4. Add mashed potatoes or pasta.

Beef Barley Soup

Ingredients:

1 pound stew beef

2 cups carrot, thinly sliced

1 cup celery, thinly sliced

3/4 cup chopped green pepper

1 cup chopped onion

1/2 cup barley

1/4 chopped parsley

3 beef bouillon cubes or equivalent beef base

2 teaspoon salt

3/4 teaspoon dried basil

2 tablespoon ketchup

Directions:

1. Place in layers in crock pot as: Vegetables, then meat, then barley and finally the remaining Ingredients; Add 5 cups of water, do not stir.
2. Cook on LOW heat for 9-10 hours
3. Serve while it's hot!

Beef Stew

Ingredients:

2 pounds stew beef
1/4 cup flour
1 teaspoon paprika
4 large carrots
3 large potatoes
1 cup condensed beef broth
1 1/2 teaspoon pepper
1/3 cups soy sauce

1 large Onion or 3-4 small yellow onions whole

8 oz canned tomato sauce

Directions:

1. Layer the potatoes, followed by carrots. Top with meat and sprinkle it with soy sauce, salt, paprika, pepper and flour. Spread with chopped onions.

2. Combined beef broth, tomato sauce and pour overall. Cover and cook on LOW heat for 7-8 hours.

Casserole

Ingredients:

1 bag (approx 32oz) frozen hash brown potatoes

1 pounds bacon

1 small onion

8 ounce shredded cheddar cheese

1/2 diced red bell pepper

1/2 diced green bell pepper

12 eggs

1 cup milk

(to taste) salt and pepper

Directions:

1. Start by cutting the bacon into small pieces and cooking it in a pan.

2. If you want to save even more time, you can use bacon that is already cooked.

3. Take your slow cooker and add half of the hash brown potatoes at the bottom.

4. Add half of the following ingredients, in this specific order: bacon, onion, red and green bell pepper and cheddar cheese.

5. This is the moment when you have to add the remaining quantity of the hash brown potatoes, continue by adding the other half of the above-mentioned ingredients.

6. Whisk the eggs together with the milk and pour over the casserole.

7. Season with salt and pepper to taste.

8. Cook for 4 hours (on low) or for 8 hours (on warm). Enjoy!

Breakfast quinoa

Ingredients:

1 cup quinoa

3 cups almond milk

4 chopped dates

1/4 cup pepitas

1 diced apple

2 tsp cinnamon

1/4 tsp nutmeg

1 tsp vanilla extract

1/4 tsp salt

Directions:

1. Start adding the quinoa, together with the rest of ingredients into slow cooker.

2. Make sure that you cook the mixture for about 3 hours, until all of the liquid has been absorbed.

3. You can also cook it overnight, for eight 8 hours on low, so as to have it ready in the morning, Just in time for breakfast. Enjoy!

Cinnamon rolls

Ingredients:

(dough)

1 1/2 cups warm water

1 tbsp active dry yeast

2 tbsp honey

3 1/2 flour

1 tsp salt

(Filling)

4 tbsp butter

1/2 cup sugar

1/4 cup brown sugar

1 tbsp cinnamon

(frosting)

2 tbsp butter

2 oz cream cheese

1 tsp vanilla

3 cups powder sugar

2-3 tbsp milk

Directions:

1. Start by mixing the warm water together with the yeast and honey into a bowl.

2. Wait for approximately 5 minutes before adding flour and salt.

3. Once the dough is ready, remove it from the bowl and let it sit for about 10 minutes, in order to rise.

4. Take another bowl and mix the regular sugar with the brown one and cinnamon, for the filling.

5. Cut the dough into pieces, spread softened butter over them and sprinkle the cinnamon-sugar mixture over them.

6. Form your cinnamon rolls and set them aside.

7. Grease your slow cooker and place the cinnamon rolls into it.

8. Cook for about 2 hours.

9. While the cinnamon rolls are cooking, prepare the frosting, by mixing the softened butter together with the cream cheese.

10. Add the vanilla and mix until you obtain a smooth mixture.

11. Add the sugar and milk gradually, making sure that they are integrated into the mixture.

12. Add the frosting to the warm cinnamon rolls and enjoy!

Chicken and potatoes and carrots

Ingredients:

1 3/4 cups onion

1 cooking spray

2 cups baby carrots

6 round red potatoes

1/2 cup chicken broth

1/2 dry white wine

1 tbsp chopped fresh thyme

1 tsp minced garlic

3/4 tsp salt

1/2 tsp fresh ground black pepper

1 tsp paprika

6 chicken thighs

1 tsp olive oil

Directions:

1. Start by applying cooking spray to the inside of the crock pot.

2. Then, add the sliced onions into the slow cooker, together with the potatoes and carrots.

3. Mix the chicken broth together with white wine, fresh thyme and garlic.

3. Add the mixture into the slow cooker.

4. Coat the chicken with a mixture of paprika, salt and pepper.

5. Brown the chicken into a pan, then place it on top of the veggies, in the slow cooker.

6. Cook for about 3 and a half hours on low heat.

7. Serve with fresh thyme as garnish. Enjoy!

Collard greens with bacon and balsamic vinegar

Ingredients:

3 bacon slices

1 cup chopped onion

1 pack/16 oz fresh collard greens

1/4 tsp salt

2 garlic cloves

1 bay leaf

1 can/ 14.5 oz chicken broth

3 tbsp balsamic vinegar

1 tbsp honey

Directions:

1. Start cooking the bacon into a pan over medium heat.

2. One crisp, cut it into small pieces or crumble it by hand.

3. For the next step, sauté the onions together with the collard greens.

4. Add the sautéed veggies into the slow cooker, together with the salt, minced garlic cloves, bay leaf and chicken broth.

5. Cook for about 4 hours on low heat.

6. Prepare the dressing by mixing the balsamic vinegar with the honey.

7. Pour the dressing and sprinkle with bacon.

8. Serve and enjoy!

Honey Ribs and Rice (Pork)

Ingredients:

2 pounds lean spare ribs

1 can condensed pork bouillon

1/2 cup water

2 tbsp maple syrup

2 tbsp honey

3 tbsp soy sauce

2 tbsp barbecue sauce

1/2 tsp dry mustard

Directions:

1. Bake at 350 degrees F around 1/2 per side or boil for about 15 to 20m minutes to remove fat.

2. Cut into single servings and combine ingredients in crock pot.

3. Add ribs and mix.

4. Cover and cook overnight or on low heat for 8 hours and serve over rice.

Chinese Pork Roast

Ingredients:

1/4 cup lower-sodium soy sauce

1/4 cup hoisin sauce

3 tbsp ketchup

3 tbsp honey

2 tsp minced garlic

2 tsp grated peeled fresh ginger

1 tsp dark sesame oil

1/2 tsp five-spice powder

1 (2 pounds) boneless pork shoulder (Boston butt), trimmed

1/2 cup fat-free, lower-sodium chicken broth

Directions:

1. Combine the first 8 ingredients in a small bowl, stir using a whisk.

2. Place it in a large zip-top plastic bag.

3. Add pork to bag and seal it.

4. Marinate in refrigerator for at least 2 hours.

5. Place the marinade pork in a electric crock pot

6. Cover and cook on low heat for 8 hours.

7. Remove the marinade pork from crock pot using a slotted spoon.

8. Cover it with an aluminum foil and keep it warm

9. Add broth in crock pot for sauce,

10. Cover and cook for at least 30 minutes or until sauce thickens.

11. Shred the pork and add the sauce

12. Serve and enjoy!

Curried Lentil-Tomato Soup (Pork)

Ingredients:

4 center-cut bacon slices

1 1/2 cups chopped sweet onion

4 garlic cloves, finely chopped

3 cups fat-free, lower-sodium chicken broth

1 cup dried lentils

1/2 cup chopped carrot

1/2 cup chopped celery

2 tsp curry powder

1/2 tsp ground ginger

1/4 tsp ground cinnamon

2 (14.5 oz) can no salted added stewed tomatoes, undrained

1/2 cup half and half

2 tbsp dry sherry

Directions:

1. Cook bacon in a large nonstick skillet over medium heat until crisp.

2. Remove bacon from pan then crumble the bacon.

3. Add onion and garlic to drippings in a pan, sauté for 3 minutes.

4. Transfer onion mixture to a 4 quart electric crock pot.

5. Add broth while stirring then add the rest of the ingredients.

6. Cover and cook on low heat for 8 hours

7. Add half and half milk and sherry while stirring.

8. Ladle soup into bowls and sprinkles with crumbled bacon.

9. Serve and enjoy!

Part 2

Introduction

You might have heard of a Keto Diet Plan, but may not have an exact idea about what it exactly is or you might be hearing it for the very first time.

Whatever category you fall into, doesn't worry, I'm here to help you. As you landed up here, it means that you have some serious interest in knowing about diet and would like to get a handy list of easy Keto Crock Pot recipes for fat loss. It's quite evident that the well-known advice to "eat less and exercise more" for weight loss is not working for all of us. It is a fact that a significant portion of dieters who lose weight, gain it back quickly. So the real question is, is there an ultimate solution to this universal problem? As per my experience and research in this area, I have come up to a conclusion that keto diet is something which can help solve this problem of weight loss.

Ketosis is significant for your weight loss as it helps suppress your appetite unlike other diets and it also provides mental clarity and increases focus. Moreover, for preparing Keto Meals, crock pots are using, which will increase the nutritional benefits like anything.

Once you get on track with Keto Diet, you no longer have to worry about your appetite. No more counting calories and no more crazy spot exercises to reduce your belly.

If this idea seems appealing to you, continue reading and get ready to be on a Keto Diet with delicious and healthy Crock Pot prepared meal plans. However, if you still have some questions, we will cover the entire upcoming chapter so that you can get started.

What is a Crock Pot?

Well, this can be a tricky question. Many people use the term "Crock Pot" to refer to a slow cooker, regardless of the brand or make. In fact, there is an official "Crock Pot", which is the slow cooker we will be using and referring to in this book.

When talking about slow cookers in general, I would describe them as a "One-Pot" appliance which allows the user to cook dishes slowly and without need for supervision. The Crock Pot is most commonly known for slow-cooked meat dishes, stews, and soups, due to the long cook time and even heat distribution.

What is the Ketogenic Diet?

Unlike many other diets, this one is easy to understand! The Ketogenic Diet is simply a high fat, low carbohydrate diet that involves reducing your intake of carbs and replacing them with fats. When you eat foods that are high in carbs, your body produces two things: insulin and glucose.

- Glucose is a molecule needed by our bodies to convert and use the energy from the food we eat to fuel our body, typically carbohydrate.
- Insulin is a substance made by our pancreas to process glucose within our bloodstream.

Since glucose is our main source of energy, the fat we have stored away is therefore not needed and sits there unused. When deciding if the Ketogenic diet is for them, many people choose a typical diet of eating foods high in carbs. We have been taught that carbs are needed for energy since we were tots. This is true, but only to point.

Despite what you may have read, there are four types of Ketogenic diet.

1. High-protein Ketogenic Diet:

This type of keto diet involves eating lots of protein. The ratio required to stick to this type of diet is 60% fat, 35% protein and 5% carbohydrates.

2. Targeted Ketogenic Diet (TKD):

If you like the freedom of having some room to move around on diet, this one is for you! You can intake more carbs if you are working out as well.

3. Cyclical Ketogenic Diet (CKD):

This type requires periods of high-carb intake-for example, 5 Ketogenic days paired with a few high-carb consumption days.

4. Standard Ketogenic Diet (SKD):

This type of keto diet is the most popular and recommended. It requires you to consume moderate amounts of protein and high amounts of fat. It is based around this popular macro; 75% fat, 20% protein and 5% carbs.

The standard Ketogenic diet is the most popular diet for beginners, but you may find that the other three diets are better suited to your body and personal goals. For now, however, I suggest that you start with the standard Ketogenic diet to see how your body adapts and to minimize any side affects you may experience on the diet. Many of my students also start with the standard diet and their weight loss results have been excellent because they have exceeded my expectations every time.

Useful Tips and Tricks for Successful Keto Diet:

Here are some hacks on how to flourish with your Ketogenic diet:

1. Super-hydrate yourself by drinking 140 to 180 oz. of water each day.
2. Exercise regularly to activate GLUT-4, a molecule that pulls sugar from the bloodstream to store as glycogen I the muscles and liver.
3. Eat fermented foods to induce good bowel motility. Constipation may hinder ketosis.
4. Create more peace and relaxation in life because chronic stress lessens the ability to maintain ketosis.
5. Get enough sleep to preserve hormones and good blood circulation.
6. Increase salt intake to 3-5 grams daily. Himalayan pink salt comes handy.
7. Use medium-chain triglyceride oil regularly as they are readily metabolized to ketone bodies.
8. Taking ketone supplements are beneficial especially at the onset of your Ketogenic journey.
9. Never exceed 20 or 30 grams of carbohydrates daily. Always count your carbs. Remember this formula: Total carbs-Fiber = Net carbs.

Be wary of eating out. Never be shy to ask for alternatives and customized meals to suit your Ketogenic diet.

How to Use the Crock Pot?

The Crock Pot is incredibly easy to use! That's part of the major appeal of this genius appliance. There are not many ways you can mess up your food with the Crock Pots, but there are some tips to follow to ensure a successful result!

1. Temperature:

Most Crock Pot models have a LOW and HIGH setting. You need to adjust your cooking time according to the temperature setting. For example, if you have the HIGH setting on, your dish might take 4 hours to cook, but if you have the LOW setting on, it might take 8 hours. Follow the guidelines in your Crock Pot handbook, and stick to the time suggestions in these recipes (and others!).

2. Size and Servings:

When purchasing your Crock Pot, choose a size that suits your regular serving needs; i.e. if you have a family of 5, choose a large pot. The thing is, you should never over-fill the Crock Pot. If you add too many ingredients, the food won't cook evenly, and it might turn out sloppy and flavorless. Don't fill the Crock Pot more than two thirds full and you'll be fine!

3. Time:

If you'd like to cook your meal throughout the day, while you are out and about, you can do so! Choose a LOW setting and cook the meal slowly, for at least 8

hours (or according to the recipe instructions). When the meal has finished cooking, the Crock Pot will automatically switch to WARM until you are ready to devour your meal.

4. Liquids:

Crock Pots and slow cookers do not reduce liquids. When you are cooking in a regular pot or pan, the liquid you add will evaporate, thicken, and reduce: this does not happen when cooking with the Crock Pot! The liquid you add at the start will be there at the end. Therefore, be careful with the amount of liquid you are adding to your dish. You can reduce and simmer liquids such as wine and cream in a pot or fry pan before you add it to the slow cooker. When using a recipe made especially for a Crock Pot or Slow Cooker, follow it carefully and you'll be perfectly fine.

What are the Benefits of Using the Crock Pot?

Anyone who owns and uses a Crock Pot will have to you about the many benefits of this appliance! Here are some of the fantastic reasons to incorporate the Crock Pot into your cooking routine:

1. Convenience:

Instead of hauling out an armful of pots and pans from the cupboards, just use the Crock Pot! It's already there on the bench, so load it up. All you need to do is clean the inner pot after you're done, and put it back into the Crock Pot unit, ready for next time.

2. Ready-to-go Meals:

A crazy lifestyle doesn't mean that you need to sacrifice wholesome and delicious meals. The amazing thing about the Crock Pot is that you can leave it to cook your meal while you are at work, or even overnight. Load the ingredients into the pot, set the temperature and time, and walk away.

3. Tender Meat:

Slow cooked meat is tender, melt-in-the-mouth, and satisfying. You can achieve this by simply throwing the meat into the pot with any flavorings you like, a small amount of liquid, and simply forget about it for hours while you live your life!

4. Versatility:

As you will see in the recipe section, you can cook anything in the Crock Pot! Meat, Vegetables, Seafood, Dessert, Starters! You can cook your dish entirely in the Crock Pot, from start to finish, or you can finish it off in a hot fry pan to give a golden crunch to meat and veggie dishes.

What to Avoid?

The Ketogenic Diet discourages the consumption of carbohydrate that is converted to glucose. Thus said, dieters are discouraged to eat high amounts of sugar and starch. These include rice, potatoes, bread, pasta, and other sugary beverages. But more than sugary foods and starches, what are other types of foods that you need to avoid when following the Ketogenic diet.

1. Sugary Foods:

Sugary foods such as cakes, candies, and ice cream should be avoided. But aside from these sinful foods, even foods that are marketed as health products are discouraged under the Ketogenic diet. These include fruit juices and sodas.

2. Root Vegetables:

Root vegetables contain high amounts of starch and must, therefore be avoided. These include carrots, parsnips, potatoes, and other types of tubers.

3. Fruits:

As mentioned earlier, fruits are discouraged under the Ketogenic diet. But if you are craving for fruits, you are limited to consuming berries like strawberries, cherries, and many others.

4. Beans:

Beans such as white beans, red beans, lentils, pulses, and basically all types of beans are discouraged with the Ketogenic diet.

5. Low Carb Products:

Many low-carb products are marketed and touted for their health benefits but not on the Ketogenic diet. You need to increase the amount of fat that you can get and dairy products, for example, are good sources. So instead of opting for low-fat milk, opt for the full-fat version.

6. Alcohol:

Specifically, beer contains high amounts of carbohydrates but distilled drinks and wine can be consumed under limited amounts.

Chicken Recipes

Comforting Chicken Stew:

Serves: 6

Preparation Time: 20 minutes

Cooking Time: 6 hours

Macros per serving:

Calories: 203

Protein: 26.9 grams

Fat: 6.8 grams

Carbohydrates: 7 grams

What you'll need:

- 3 cups carrots, peeled and cubed
- ½ cup yellow onion, chopped
- 2 garlic cloves, minced
- Salt and freshly ground black pepper, to taste
- ¼ teaspoon dried thyme
- ½ teaspoon dried sage
- 3 (6-ounce) grass-fed, boneless chicken breasts, cubed
- 2 cups homemade chicken broth

How to make it:

1. In a large Crockpot, add all ingredients except cilantro and stir to combine.
2. Set the Crockpot on low and cook, covered, for about 7-8 hours
3. Serve hot.

Crock Pot Balsamic Boneless Chicken Thighs:

Serves: 8

Preparation Time: 5 minutes

Cooking Time: 4 hours

Macros per serving:

Calories: 133

Protein: 20.1 grams

Fat: 4 grams

Carbohydrates: 5.6 grams

What you'll need:
- 1 teaspoon Ground garlic
- 1 teaspoon Basil dried
- ½ teaspoon Salt
- ½ teaspoon Pepper

- 2 teaspoons Onion, dried & minced
- 4 Minced garlic cloves
- 1 tablespoon Olive oil, extra virgin
- ½ cup Balsamic vinegar
- 8 Chicken thighs boneless and skinless (about 24 ounces)
- Fresh chopped parsley

How to make it:

1. Take a medium bowl and mix the all dry spices and paste all over the chicken.
2. Pour one tablespoon olive oil to the Crockpot.
3. Add garlic.
4. Place the chicken.
5. You can dispense the balsamic vinegar on the chicken and make sure it reaches everywhere on the chicken.
6. Cover the crockpot and cook on high about 4 hours.
7. Once cooking over, transfer the dish to a serving bowl.
8. Sprinkle fresh on top the chicken.
9. Serve and enjoy.

Chicken Tikka Masala:

Serves: 2

Preparation Time: 15 minutes

Cooking Time: 6 hours

Macros per serving:

Calories: 493

Protein: 46 grams

Fat: 41.2 grams

Carbohydrates: 5.8 grams

What you'll need:
- 1 lb. chicken thighs, de-boned and chopped into bite-sized
- 3 teaspoons gram masala
- ½ cup heavy cream

- ½ cup coconut milk
- 1 teaspoon onion powder
- 2 minced cloves of garlic
- 1 teaspoon paprika
- 2 teaspoons salt

How to make it:

1. Put chicken to Crockpot and add grated ginger knob on top. Also add the seasonings: 1 teaspoon onion powder, 2 minced cloves of garlic, 1 teaspoon paprika and 2 teaspoons salt. Mix.
2. Add tomatoes and coconut oil. Mix.
3. Cook for 6 hours on low.
4. When cooked, add heavy cream to chicken the curry.

Flavorful Chicken and Gravy:

Serves: 6

Preparation Time: 10 minutes

Cooking Time: 8 hours

Macros per serving:

Calories: 323

Protein: 44.9 grams

Fat: 12 grams

Carbohydrates: 6.2 grams

What you'll need:

- 2 lbs. chicken breasts, skinless, boneless and cut into pieces
- 3 cups chicken stock
- 1 oz. brown gravy mix

- 1 oz. onion soup mix

How to make it:

1. Add chicken stock, brown gravy mix, and onion soup mix into the slow cooker and stir well.
2. Add chicken into the slow cooker.
3. Cover and cook on low for 8 hours.
4. Stir well and serve.

Lemon Grass and Coconut Chicken:

Serves: 6

Preparation Time: 20 minutes

Cooking Time: 5 hours

Macros per serving:

Calories: 455

Protein: 40.89 grams

Fat: 29.57 grams

Carbohydrates: 5.38 grams

What you'll need:

- 10 chicken drumsticks, skin removed
- Salt and pepper to taste
- 1 stalk of lemongrass, trimmed
- 4 cloves of garlic, minced
- 1 pieces ginger, sliced thinly
- 1 cup coconut milk
- 3 tablespoons coconut aminos
- 2 tablespoons fish sauce
- 1 teaspoon five spice powder
- 1 green onion, chopped

How to make it:

1. In a large bowl, season the chicken drumstick with salt and pepper.
2. Place the lemongrass, garlic, ginger, coconut milk, coconut aminos, fish sauce, and five-spice powder in a blender or food processor. Blend until smooth.
3. Place the chicken in the slow cooker and pour over the marinade. Mix well.
4. Set the Crockpot to low and cook for 4 to 5 hours.
5. Once done, serve with green onions.

Indian Chicken Curry:

Serves: 6

Preparation Time: 20 minutes

Cooking Time: 5 hours 5 minutes

Macros per serving:

Calories: 426

Protein: 50.8 grams

Fat: 17.5 grams

Carbohydrates: 11.6 grams

What you'll need:
- 2 pounds grass-fed, bone-in chicken thighs
- Salt and freshly ground black pepper, to taste
- 1 small yellow onion, chopped roughly

- 3 garlic cloves, chopped roughly
- 1 teaspoon fresh ginger, chopped roughly
- 1 tablespoon curry powder
- ¼ cup water
- 2 tablespoons olive oil
- 1 cup cherry tomatoes, halved
- 1 ¼ cups plain yogurt, whipped
- ¼ cup fresh cilantro
- 1 tablespoon fresh lemon juice

How to make it:

1. Season chicken thighs with salt and black pepper evenly.
2. In a food processor, add onion, garlic, ginger, water, and curry powder and pulse until smooth.
3. In a frying pan, heat oil and sauté onion mixture for about 3-5 minutes.
4. In a large Crockpot, place chicken thighs with sautéed onion mixture, tomatoes, and yogurt and stir to combine.
5. Set the Crockpot on low and cook, covered, for about 5 hours.
6. Stir in cilantro and lemon juice and serve hot.

Crock Pot Chicken Lo Mein:

Serves: 6

Preparation Time: 10 minutes

Cooking Time: 4 hours

Macros per serving:

Calories: 174

Protein: 24.5 grams

Fat: 10.2 grams

Carbohydrates: 3.1 grams

What you'll need:
- 1 ½ pounds Chicken sliced
- 1 bunch Napa cabbage washed
- 12 ounces Low carb noodles
- 1 teaspoon Clove garlic, minced
- Salt to taste

- Pepper as required

For Marinating:

- 1 tablespoon Tamari/soy aminos
- ½ teaspoon Garlic paste
- ½ teaspoon Sesame oil

For making sauce:

- ¾ cup Chicken broth
- 1 tablespoon Sweetener
- ¼ cup Tamari/soy aminos
- 1 tablespoon Vinegar
- 2 teaspoons Sesame oil
- 1 teaspoon Pepper chili flakes
- ½ teaspoon Thickener (optional)

How to make it:

1. Marinate the chicken using the ingredients and keep it in the fridge for setting about 30 minutes. Use a small bowl to marinate.
2. Clean the Crockpot and coat slightly with non-stick oil.
3. Put the marinated chicken in the cooker and start cooking in slow heat for about 2 hours.
4. Stir it intermittently and also check the tenderness of the chicken.
5. Once done, remove the chicken from the cooker and put garlic, ginger, and vegetables into the cooker and place the cooked chicken on top of it.
6. Now it is time for making the sauce.

7. Mix all the sauce ingredients in a bowl and transfer everything to the cooker.
8. Continue cook for about 2 hours and stir intermittently.
9. Ten minutes before winding up the cooking, rinse the noodle and keep it ready.
10. Transfer the washed and soaked noodles into the cooker.
11. Cover the noodles with the sauce by using tongs.
12. Add the thickener if required.
13. Just pot the Crockpot to a high temperature for about 15 minutes.
14. Serve hot

Roasted Chicken with Lemon & Parsley Butter:

Serves: 2

Preparation Time: 5 minutes

Cooking Time: 8 hours

Macros per serving:

Calories: 300

Protein: 29 grams

Fat: 18 grams

Carbohydrates: 1 gram

What you'll need:
- 4 lb. chicken, any part
- 1 whole lemon, sliced
- 2 tablespoons butter or ghee
- 1 tablespoon parsley, chopped

How to make it:

1. Rub chicken all over with salt and pepper to taste. Put in the Crockpot and pour 1 cup of water.
2. Cover and cook for 3 hours on high.
3. When cooked, add the lemon slices butter and parsley to the Crockpot.
4. Cook and cover for another 10 minutes.

Tender Cilantro Lime Chicken:

Serves: 12

Preparation Time: 10 minutes

Cooking Time: 6 hours

Macros per serving:

Calories: 162

Protein: 22.4 grams

Fat: 5.9 grams

Carbohydrates: 4.5 grams

What you'll need:

- 6 chicken breast, boneless
- 2 jalapeno peppers, chopped
- 1.25 oz. taco seasoning
- ¼ cup fresh cilantro, chopped
- 1 lime juice
- 24 oz. salsa

How to make it:

1. Add all ingredients except chicken into the slow cooker and mix well.
2. Add chicken into the slow cooker.
3. Cover and cook on low for 6 hours.
4. Shred chicken using a fork and serve.

Keto Jerk Chicken:

Serves: 4

Preparation Time: 10 minutes

Cooking Time: 5 hours

Macros per serving:

Calories: 281

Protein: 30.24 grams

Fat: 15.38 grams

Carbohydrates: 4.31 grams

What you'll need:
- 4 teaspoons paprika
- 4 teaspoons salt
- 1 teaspoon cayenne pepper
- 2 teaspoons thyme
- 2 teaspoons onion powder

- 2 teaspoons garlic powder
- 1 teaspoon black pepper
- 5 chicken drumsticks, skin removed

How to make it:

1. Make a spice rub by combining in bowl paprika, salt, cayenne pepper, thyme, onion powder, garlic powder, and black pepper.
2. Coat the chicken with the spice rub and place inside the Crockpot.
3. Set the temperature to low heat and cook for 6 hours or until the chicken meat falls off the bone.

Sweet and Tangy Chicken:

Serves: 6

Preparation Time: 15 minutes

Cooking Time: 8 hours

Macros per serving:

Calories: 254

Protein: 37.4 grams

Fat: 9.6 grams

Carbohydrates: 6 grams

What you'll need:

- 1 medium yellow onion, chopped
- 1/3 cup chives, minced
- 1 tablespoon fresh ginger, minced
- 3 tablespoons fresh lemon juice
- 2 tablespoons erythritol
- 2 tablespoons water
- 1 ½ tablespoons soy sauce
- ½ teaspoon red pepper flakes
- 2 ½ pounds grass-fed boneless chicken breasts, cut into pieces

How to make it:

1. In a bowl, add all ingredients except chicken and blend well.
2. Place chicken pieces in the bottom of a Crockpot and top evenly with onion mixture.
3. Set the Crockpot on low and cook, covered for about 6-8 hours.
4. Serve hot

Slow Cooker Moscow Chicken:

Serves: 6

Preparation Time: 10-15 minutes

Cooking Time: 6 hours

Macros per serving:

Calories: 150.7

Protein: 14.9 grams

Fat: 2.8 grams

Carbohydrates: 10.8 grams

What you'll need:
- 6 Chicken thighs
- ½ teaspoon Grated ginger
- 6 Bacon, sliced

- 10 ounces Russian salad dressing
- 2 Clove garlic, chopped
- 2 Onion, chopped
- Pepper as required
- Salt to taste

How to make it:

1. Take a large skillet and heat on medium temperature.
2. Put chicken and cook it until both sides become brown.
3. Let it cool after done.
4. Now warp the chicken thighs in bacon and put it into the slow cooker.
5. Spread ginger and garlic over the chicken.
6. Top it with Russian salad.
7. Cook for 5-6 hours
8. Once ready, season it with pepper and salt.

Greek Chicken

Serves: 2

Preparation Time: 5 minutes

Cooking Time: 6 hours

Macros per serving:

Calories: 396

Protein: 28.7 grams

Fat: 29.8 grams

Carbohydrates: 4 grams

What you'll need:
- 2 chicken breast, skinless
- 1 ½ tablespoon Greek Rub
- 1 ½ tablespoons lemon juice
- 1 chicken bouillon cube dissolved in water

How to make it:

1. Coat each breast with Greek rub, and then rub with garlic powder.
2. Put the chicken breasts in the Crockpot and spray with lemon juice.
3. Pour the chicken bouillon mixture in the Crockpot.
4. Cook for 6 hours on low.

Delicious Butter Chicken:

Serves: 8

Preparation Time: 10 minutes

Cooking Time: 6 hours 30 minutes

Macros per serving:

Calories: 374

Protein: 37.5 grams

Fat: 22.5 grams

Carbohydrates: 5.3 grams

What you'll need:

- 2.2 lbs. chicken thighs, skinless
- 1 cup coconut milk
- 1 cup tomatoes, crushed
- 4 tablespoons butter
- 2 teaspoons curry powder
- 2 teaspoons ground cumin
- 2 teaspoons ground paprika
- 3 teaspoons ground cinnamon
- 1 medium onion, chopped
- 1 teaspoon salt

How to make it:

1. Add onion into the slow cooker then place chicken on top of onion.
2. Sprinkle all spices on top of chicken.
3. Pour crushed tomatoes on top of chicken.
4. Cover and cook on low for 6 hours.
5. Add coconut milk and cook for one more half-hour.
6. Stir well and serve.

Easy-Breezy Fajita Chicken:

Serves: 8

Preparation Time: 10 minutes

Cooking Time: 6 hours

Macros per serving:

Calories: 151

Protein: 26.18 grams

Fat: 3.13 grams

Carbohydrates: 3.44 grams

What you'll need:
- 2 pounds boneless chicken breast, skin removed
- 1 small onion, sliced thinly
- 4 cloves of garlic, minced
- 2 cups bell pepper, sliced
- 1 can diced tomatoes
- 1 teaspoon salt

- 1 teaspoon oregano
- 1 teaspoon coriander, ground
- ½ teaspoon cumin
- ½ teaspoon chili powder

How to make it:

1. Place the chicken at the bottom of the Crockpot and add the onions, garlic and bell peppers.
2. Pour over the diced tomatoes.
3. Stir in the rest of the ingredients.
4. Cook at the low-temperature setting for 6 hours.

Beef Recipes

Soul Warming Beef Stew:

Serves: 8

Preparation Time: 15 minutes

Cooking Time: 9 hours

Macros per serving:

Calories: 248

Protein: 36.5 grams

Fat: 7.4 grams

Carbohydrates: 7.4 grams

What you'll need:

- 1 medium head cabbage, roughly chopped (485 g)
- 1 medium yellow onion, chopped
- 6 garlic cloves, minced
- 2 pounds grass-fed beef stew meat, cubed
- 2 cups tomatoes, chopped finely
- Salt and freshly ground black pepper, to taste
- 1 cup homemade beef broth

How to make it:

1. In a large Crockpot, add all ingredients and stir to combine.
2. Set the Crockpot on low and cook, covered, for about 9 hours.
3. Serve hot.

Crockpot – Low Carb Short Beef Ribs:

Serves: 12

Preparation Time: 15 minutes

Cooking Time: 4 hours

Macros per serving:

Calories: 489

Protein: 16 grams

Fat: 42 grams

Carbohydrates: 3 grams

What you'll need:
- 4 pounds Beef with short ribs or boneless
- 1 ½ cups Onion, chopped
- 1 cup Beef broth
- 2 tablespoons Olive oil

- 2 tablespoons Worcestershire sauce or ordinary homemade
- 2 tablespoons Tomato paste
- 3 No's Garlic clove, minced
- Salt to taste
- Pepper to taste
- 1 ½ cups Red wine
- Celery, carrots – optional

How to make it:

1. In a large skillet, pour oil and heat on medium temperature.
2. Season the ribs, one side with salt and pepper.
3. Put half of the ribs, facing the seasoned into the hot oil.
4. Flip it once the side becomes brown.
5. Remove and set aside.
6. Continue the remaining.
7. Take a 4-quart Crockpot and place short ribs into it.
8. In the skillet put the remaining ingredients and boil it.
9. Cook until the onion becomes tender.
10. Transfer it to the Crockpot.
11. Cover and continue cooking for 8-10 hours.

Braised Corned beef Brisket:

Serves: 2

Preparation Time: 15 minutes

Cooking Time: 6 hours 15 minutes

Macros per serving:

Calories: 455

Protein: 30.6 grams

Fat: 33.7 grams

Carbohydrates: 5.4 grams

What you'll need:
- 1/3 tablespoon vegetable oil
- 1/3 flat-cut corned beef brisket
- 1/3 tablespoon browning sauce

How to make it:

1. Prepare seasonings: 1/3 sliced onion and 2 sliced garlic cloves.
2. Apply a generous amount of browning sauce to both sides of the brisket.
3. In a skillet, cook the brisket in preheated vegetable oil for 5-8 minutes on both sides.
4. Place the brisket in a crock-pot. Scatter the seasonings and add a tablespoon of water.
5. Cover and cook for 6 hours on low.

Chili Lime Shredded Beef:

Serves: 6

Preparation Time: 10 minutes

Cooking Time: 8 hours

Macros per serving:

Calories: 563

Protein: 40.2 grams

Fat: 42.5 grams

Carbohydrates: 2.5 grams

What you'll need:

- 2 lb. beef chuck roast
- 2 lime juice
- 3 garlic cloves, crushed
- 1 teaspoon chili powder
- 4 cups chicken stock
- 1 teaspoon salt

How to make it:

1. Place chuck roast into the bottom of slow cooker.
2. Pour chicken stock over chuck roast
3. Season roast with chili powder, garlic, and salt.
4. Cover and cook on low for 8 hours.
5. Shred chuck roast using a fork and pour lime juice over shredded meat.
6. Serve hot and enjoy.

Exotic Middle Eastern Beef:

Serves: 8

Preparation Time: 20 minutes

Cooking Time: 8 hours

Macros per serving:

Calories: 563

Protein: 40.91 grams

Fat: 40.86 grams

Carbohydrates: 5.14 grams

What you'll need:
- 3 pounds beef brisket
- Salt and pepper to taste
- 1 teaspoon fennel seeds
- 1 teaspoon whole peppercorns

- 1 teaspoon cumin powder
- 1 teaspoon cardamom powder
- ½ teaspoon ground cinnamon
- 3 tablespoons tomato paste
- ½ onion, chopped
- 3 cups bone broth
- ¼ cup coconut vinegar

How to make it:
1. Place all ingredients in the pot.
2. Cook at low temperature for 8 hours.
3. Once cooked, shred with a fork.

Richly Taste Beef Chili:

Serves: 12

Preparation Time: 20 minutes

Cooking Time: 7 hours

Macros per serving:

Calories: 303

Protein: 41.2 grams

Fat: 10.7 grams

Carbohydrates: 10.9 grams

What you'll need:

- 3 pounds ground lean grass-fed beef
- 1 large yellow onion, chopped
- Salt and freshly ground black pepper, to taste
- 1 (10-ounces) package Portobello mushrooms, sliced
- 1 (28-ounce) can fire-roasted tomatoes with juice
- 2 jalapeno peppers, seeded and chopped finely
- 1 tablespoon garlic, minced
- 3 tablespoons capers
- ¼ cup sugar-free tomato paste
- 1 cup homemade beef broth
- 2 tablespoons dried thyme, crushed
- 2 tablespoons ground cumin
- 1 tablespoon ground cinnamon
- 3 tablespoons red chili powder
- 1 tablespoon cayenne pepper
- ½ tablespoon erythritol
- 2 tablespoons balsamic vinegar
- 1 ¼ cups parmesan cheese, grated freshly
- 2 cups scallions, chopped

How to make it:

1. In a large Crockpot, add beef, onion, salt, and black pepper and stir well.
2. Set the Crockpot on low and cook, covered, for about 3 hours, stirring occasionally.
3. Uncover the Crockpot and drain the grease completely.
4. Add remaining ingredients except for parmesan cheese and scallion and mix well.
5. Set the Crockpot on low and cook, covered, for about 3-4 hours
6. Serve hot with the topping of cheese and scallion.

Mexican Crockpot Beef Roast:

Serves: 10

Preparation Time: 15 minutes

Cooking Time: 7 hours

Macros per serving:

Calories: 608

Protein: 44 grams

Fat: 3 grams

Carbohydrates: 7 grams

What you'll need:

- 3 ½ pounds Beef chuck arm
- 1 teaspoon Cumin, grounded
- 2 teaspoons Garlic, minced
- 1 teaspoon Black pepper, ground
- 2 tablespoons Tomato paste
- ½ teaspoon Coriander, grounded
- 2 cups Fresh salsa
- 3 tablespoons Bacon grease
- 2 cups Beef broth
- 2 tablespoons Sauce
- Salt to taste

How to make it:

1. Season the beef with grounded black pepper and spices.
2. Take a heavy skillet and over medium-high heat, melt the bacon grease.
3. Roast it until becoming brown on all sides.
4. Put all the roasted beef in the crockpot.
5. Add tomato paste, sauce and salsa over the meet.
6. Add beef broth.
7. Put the remaining bacon grease and any other leftovers over the beef.
8. Cover the cook on low heat.
9. Depending on the meet, you need to cook it for 6-8 hours on slow cooking.
10. Once the cooking is over, remove the beef to a large bowl and pull the meat into small rags, when it is

cool. You can do it by hand or with forks. Remove excess fat if anything is there.
11. Once done, serve hot.

Italian Beef for Sandwiches:

Serves: 2

Preparation Time: 15 minutes

Cooking Time: 5 hours

Macros per serving:

Calories: 318

Protein: 39.4 grams

Fat: 15.8 grams

Carbohydrates: 1.6 grams

What you'll need:

- ¼ bay leaf
- ¼ (0.7 oz.) package dry Italian – style salad dressing mix
- ¼ teaspoon dried parsley
- ¼ teaspoon dried oregano
- ¼ (5 lb.) rump roast

How to make it:

1. Prepare to the season: ½ cup water with salt, garlic powder, and ground black pepper to taste.
2. Add the seasonings to the salad dressing mix.
3. Add the bay leaf, parsley, and oregano. Mix well.
4. Put the roast in the crock-pot and pour the resulting salad dressing mixture. Mix well.
5. Cover and cook for four to five hours on high.

Tasty Pulled Beef:

Serves: 12

Preparation Time: 10 minutes

Cooking Time: 8 hours 30 minutes

Macros per serving:

Calories: 582

Protein: 40.4 grams

Fat: 42.6 grams

Carbohydrates: 6.8 grams

What you'll need:
- 4 lbs. beef chuck roast
- 1 teaspoon onion powder
- 2 tablespoons chili powder
- 1 tablespoon paprika
- 2 garlic cloves, minced
- 1 tablespoon Dijon mustard

- 1 cup ketchup
- 1 cup balsamic vinegar
- 2 cups chicken stock
- Pepper
- Salt

How to make it:

1. In a bowl, combine together paprika. Garlic, onion powder, chili powder, pepper, and salt.
2. Rub spice mixture all over beef roasted and place in the slow cooker.
3. Pour chicken stock over roast. Cover slow cookware with lid and cook on low for eight hours.
4. Add ketchup, vinegar, mustard, pepper, and salt in a saucepan and heat over medium heat. Bring to boil and let simmer for ten minutes.
5. Remove beef roast from slow cooker and shred using a fork.
6. Return shredded meat into the slow cooker and pour ketchup mixture over shredded meat.
7. Stir well and cook on high for 30 minutes more.
8. Serve and enjoy.

Pepper Beef Tongue Stew:

Serves: 10

Preparation Time: 15 minutes

Cooking Time: 8 hours

Macros per serving:

Calories: 441

Protein: 28.57 grams

Fat: 31.07 grams

Carbohydrates: 9.3 grams

What you'll need:
- 3 pounds sliced beef tongue, boiled and cleaned
- 1 Onion, chopped
- 6 cloves of garlic, minced
- 1 red bell pepper, diced

- 1 yellow bell pepper, diced
- 2 cups chicken stock
- 8-ounce can of tomato sauce
- 2 jalapeno peppers, diced
- Salt and pepper to taste
- 1 teaspoon Cajun spice
- 1 ¾ stick of butter
- 1 bunch of green onion, chopped

How to make it:

1. Place the beef tongue, onion, garlic, and bell peppers in the Crockpot.
2. Add the chicken stock and tomato sauce. Stir in the jalapeno pepper and season with salt, pepper and Cajun spice.
3. Cook on low temperature for 8 hours.
4. Once cooked, add butter and garnish with green onions.

Sweet & Tangy Beef Shoulder:

Serves: 14

Preparation Time: 15 minutes

Cooking Time: 9 hours 10 minutes

Macros per serving:

Calories: 516

Protein: 48.4 grams

Fat: 33.1 grams

Carbohydrates: 1.1 grams

What you'll need:
- ¼ cup unsalted butter
- 8 pounds grass-fed chuck shoulder roast
- Salt and freshly ground black pepper, to taste
- 1 yellow onion, chopped
- 4 garlic cloves, minced
- 1 tablespoon Dijon mustard

- 2 tablespoons vinegar
- 2 tablespoons fresh lemon juice
- 3-4 drops liquid stevia

How to make it:

1. In a large skillet, melt butter over medium-high heat and cook beef with salt and black pepper for about 1-2 minutes per side.
2. Transfer the beef into a large Crockpot.
3. In the same skillet, add onion and sauté for about 2-3 minutes.
4. Place onion evenly over beef.
5. In a bowl, mix together remaining ingredients.
6. Pour the sauce evenly over beef.
7. Set the Crockpot on low and cook, covered, for about 9 hours.
8. Uncover the Crockpot and transfer the beef to a cutting board.
9. Transfer the sauce into a small pan over medium-high heat and cook for about 5 minutes or until desired thickness.
10. Cut beef shoulder into desired sized slices.
11. Pour sauce over beef slices and serve.

Ronaldo's Beef Carnitas:

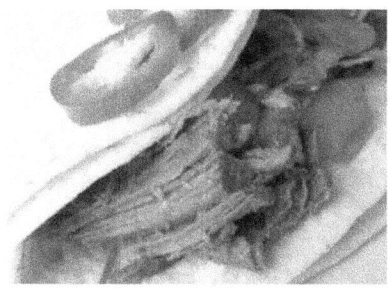

Serves: 2

Preparation Time: 5 minutes

Cooking Time: 8 hours

Macros per serving:

Calories: 218

Protein: 20.8 grams

Fat: 13.8 grams

Carbohydrates: 1.4 grams

What you'll need:
- 11 oz. chuck roast
- 1/8 can green chili peppers, chopped
- 1 teaspoon chili powder
- 1/8 teaspoon dried oregano
- 1/8 teaspoon ground cumin

How to make it:

1. Prepare the seasonings: mix all ingredients except the chuck roast. Add salt and pepper to taste.
2. Rub the mixture generously on the chuck roast and cover with aluminum foil. Put in the crock-pot.
3. Cover and cook for concerning eight hours on low.

Smokey Beef Brisket:

Serves: 6

Preparation Time: 10 minutes

Cooking Time 8 hours

Macros per serving:

Calories: 297

Protein: 46.5 grams

Fat: 9.8 grams

Carbohydrates: 2.2 grams

What you'll need:

- 2 lbs. beef brisket
- 3 tablespoons chili sauce
- ¼ cup chicken broth
- 1 ½ teaspoons liquid smoke
- ½ teaspoon pepper
- 1 teaspoon cumin
- 1 tablespoon Worcestershire sauce
- 1 tablespoon chili powder
- 3 garlic cloves, chopped
- ½ onion, chopped

How to make it:

1. In a small bowl, mix together chili powder, pepper, cumin, Worcestershire sauce, and garlic.
2. Rub chili powder mixture all over the beef brisket and place brisket into the slow cooker.
3. Mix together broth, chili sauce, onion, and liquid smoke and pour over brisket.
4. Cover and cook on low for 8 hours.
5. Remove brisket from slow cooker and slice and serve.

Indian Beef Stew

Serves: 8

Preparation Time: 20 minutes

Cooking Time: 8 hours

Macros per serving:

Calories: 134

Protein: 15.96 grams

Fat: 4.88 grams

Carbohydrates: 3.48 grams

What you'll need:

- ½ tablespoon oil
- 2 ½ pounds beef chunks

- 1 onion, diced
- 1 can tomatoes
- 2 cups beef stock
- 2 teaspoons ginger paste
- 2 teaspoons garlic, minced
- 2 tablespoons curry powder
- 2 teaspoons gram masala powder
- ¼ teaspoon ground cloves
- 2 bay leaves
- ¼ cup whipping cream
- ½ cup Greek yogurt

How to make it:

1. In a skillet, heat oil and sear the beef chunks. Set aside.
2. Place all ingredients in the Crockpot except the whipping cream and yogurt.
3. Add the seared beef chunks.
4. Close the lid and cook on low for eight hours.
5. Add the cream and yogurt before serving.

Divine Beef Shanks

Serves: 10

Preparation Time: 15 minutes

Cooking Time: 8 hours 10 minutes

Macros per serving:

Calories: 513

Protein: 77.9 grams

Fat: 18.9 grams

Carbohydrates: 3.2 grams

What you'll need:
- 3 tablespoons unsalted butter
- 5 (1-pound) grass-fed beef shanks
- Salt and freshly ground black pepper, to taste
- 1 large yellow onion, chopped

- 10 garlic cloves, minced
- 2 tablespoons sugar-free tomato paste
- 4 fresh rosemary sprigs
- 4 fresh thyme sprigs
- 2 cups homemade beef broth

How to make it:

1. In a large skillet, melt butter over medium-high heat and cook beef shanks with salt and black pepper for about 4-5 minutes per side.
2. Transfer the beef shanks to a large Crockpot.
3. In the same skillet, sauté onion for about 3-4 minutes.
4. Add garlic and sauté for about 1 minute.
5. Place onion mixture over beef shanks and cover evenly with tomato paste.
6. With a kitchen string, tie the herbs sprigs.
7. Arrange tied sprigs over tomato paste and pour broth on top evenly.
8. Set the Crockpot on low and cook, covered, for about 8 hours.
9. Serve hot.

Lamb Recipes

Keto Lamb Barbacoa:

Serves: 10

Preparation Time: 10 minutes

Cooking Time: 6 hours

Macros per serving:

Calories: 492

Protein: 38 grams

Fat: 36 grams

Carbohydrates: 1.2 grams

What you'll need:

- 5 ½ pounds Boneless leg of lamb
- ¼ cup Dried mustard
- 2 tablespoons Himalayan salt
- 2 tablespoons Smoked paprika
- 1 tablespoon Grounded cumin
- 1 tablespoon Dried oregano
- 1 tablespoon Chipotle powder
- 1 cup Water

How to make it:

1. Take a small mixing bowl and add oregano, salt, paprika, cumin, and chipotle powder and mix everything properly.
2. Now coat the lamb with mustard and spread the spice you mixed in the bowl evenly on the lamb.
3. Place the marinated lamb in a slow cooker and add water to it.
4. Let it cook for six hours.
5. Shred the lamb with a fork after cooking.
6. Leave only one cup of water in the lamb and drain out the rest of the water.

Greek Lamb Roast:

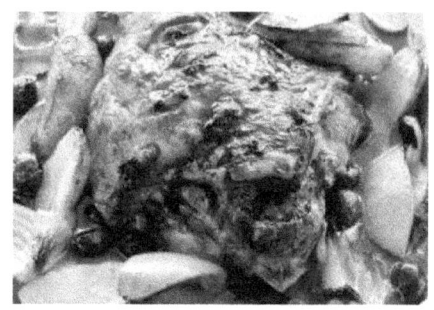

Serves: 2

Preparation Time: 10 minutes

Cooking Time: 4 hours

Macros per serving:

Calories: 443

Protein: 31 grams

Fat: 20 grams

Carbohydrates: 3 grams

What you'll need:

- 1 lemon
- 1 ¾ lb. leg of lamb, browned
- 2 teaspoons paprika
- 1 teaspoon dried oregano
- 1 cup chicken stock

How to make it:

1. Place lamb in Crock-Pot and add paprika, oregano, bay leaves (if desired), lemon juice and salt and pepper to taste.
2. Add the chicken stock and mix.
3. Cover and cook for 4 hours on high.
4. Use a spoon to scrape off undesired fat deposits to the meat.

Tasty Lamb Shoulders:

Serves: 4

Preparation Time: 10 minutes

Cooking Time: 4 hours

Macros per serving:

Calories: 441

Protein: 64.5 grams

Fat: 16.8 grams

Carbohydrates: 2.8 grams

What you'll need:

- 2 lbs. lamb shoulder
- ¼ cup beef broth
- ¼ cup fresh mint
- ¼ cup onion, chopped
- ¼ lb. carrots
- 2 tablespoons spice rub

How to make it:

1. Pour beef broth into the slow cooker.
2. Rub spice on all over lamb shoulder and place lamb shoulder into the slow cooker.
3. Add remaining ingredients into the slow cooker.
4. Cover and cook on high for 4 hours.
5. Shred the meat using a fork.
6. Serve and enjoy.

Island Lamb Stew:

Serves: 4

Preparation Time: 15 minutes

Cooking Time: 8 hours

Macros per serving:

Calories: 352

Protein: 29.32 grams

Fat: 22.4 grams

Carbohydrates: 7.83 grams

What you'll need:

- 1 tablespoon butter
- 1 cup onion, sliced
- 1 pound lamb, diced
- 1 cup celery, sliced

- ¾ cup green pepper, chopped
- 1 tablespoon curry powder
- 1 can tomatoes
- Salt and pepper to taste

How to make it:
1. Set the Crockpot to high heat and add butter.
2. Sauté the onions for a minute then add the lamb.
3. Sear the lamb for 3 minutes.
4. Pour the remaining ingredients.
5. Close the lid and set the warmth to low.
6. Cook for 8 hours.

Basic Lamb Stew:

Serves: 2

Preparation Time: 5 minutes

Cooking Time: 3 hours

Macros per serving:

Calories: 380

Protein: 58 grams

Fat: 12 grams

Carbohydrates: 9 grams

What you'll need:

- 1 lb. boneless lamb stewing meat
- 8 oz. turnips, peeled and chopped
- 8 oz. mushrooms, sliced or quartered
- 14 oz. can of beef broth

How to make it:

1. Add all ingredients in a crock-pot. Also add seasonings: onion and garlic powder, salt and pepper to taste.
2. Cover and cook for 3 hours on high, or for 6 hours on low.
3. Check for seasoning additional} and add more if required.

Thyme Lamb Chops:

Serves: 2

Preparation Time: 10 minutes

Cooking Time: 6 hours

Macros per serving:

Calories: 257

Protein: 25.1 grams

Fat: 10.1 grams

Carbohydrates: 6.4 grams

What you'll need:
- 2 lamb shoulder chops, bone in
- ¼ cup fresh thyme
- 1 teaspoon garlic paste
- ½ cup red wine

- 1 cup beef broth
- Pepper
- Salt

How to make it:

1. Add all ingredients into the slow cooker and mix well.
2. Cover and cook on low for 6 hours.
3. Serve and enjoy.

Garlic Lamb Roast:

Serves: 2

Preparation Time: 10 minutes

Cooking Time: 10 hours

Macros per serving:

Calories: 435

Protein: 44 grams

Fat: 31 grams

Carbohydrates: 6 grams

What you'll need:
- 2 tablespoons coconut vinegar
- 1 teaspoon rosemary
- 1 leg of lamb
- 2 tablespoons Worcestershire sauce
- Desired veggies: chopped carrots, onions, and butternut squash

How to make it:
1. Put all ingredients in crock-pot. Add seasonings such as garlic, pepper, and salt to taste.
2. Cook on low for 6-10 hours or until the lamb is tender.

Garlic Herbed Lamb Chops:

Serves: 4

Preparation Time: 10 minutes

Cooking Time: 4 hours

Macros per serving:

Calories: 656

Protein: 38.5 grams

Fat: 52.1 grams

Carbohydrates: 3.7 grams

What you'll need:
- 8 lamb loin chops
- 2 garlic cloves, minced
- 1/8 teaspoon black pepper
- ½ teaspoon garlic powder

- ½ teaspoon dried thyme
- 1 teaspoon dried oregano
- 1 medium onion, sliced
- ¼ teaspoon salt

How to make it:

1. In a small bowl, mix together oregano, garlic powder, thyme, pepper, and salt.
2. Rub herb mixture over the lamb chops.
3. Place lamb chops into the slow cooker.
4. Top lamb chops with garlic and sliced onion.
5. Cover and cook on low for 4 hours.
6. Serve and enjoy.

Tamil Attukal Paya Dish:

Serves: 10

Preparation Time: 10 minutes

Cooking Time: 10 hours

Macros per serving:

Calories: 184

Protein: 17.06 grams

Fat: 11.51 grams

Carbohydrates: 2.27 grams

What you'll need:

- 1 ½ pounds lamb fee, cut into chunks
- 1 onion, chopped
- 3 cloves of garlic
- 1 teaspoon black peppercorns
- 1-inch ginger, sliced thinly
- 1 can tomatoes
- 1 teaspoon coriander, ground
- ½ teaspoon cayenne pepper powder
- 1 bay leaf
- 4 cups water

How to make it:

1. Broil the lamb fee first in the oven for 10 minutes to add a roasted flavor on the soup.
2. Meanwhile, mix all other ingredients except the bay leaf and water in a food processor and pulse until fine.
3. Place the lamb feet in the Crockpot and pour over the sauce.
4. Add the bay leaf and water.

5. Cook on low for 10 hours.

Lamb Shanks with Tomatoes:

Serves: 2

Preparation Time: 15 minutes

Cooking Time: 8 hours

Macros per serving:

Calories: 397

Protein: 29 grams

Fat: 34 grams

Carbohydrates: 5 grams

What you'll need:
- 1/3 tablespoon tomato paste
- 1 x 400g tin diced tomatoes

- 1/3 tablespoon sundried tomato pesto
- 1/3 cup beef stock
- 2 lb. lamb shanks

How to make it:

1. Heat oil in a saucepan and cook onions until translucent. Add garlic and cook for 3 minutes.
2. Add ingredient and cook for an additional a pair of minutes, stirring.
3. Add diced tomatoes, sundried tomato pesto, and broth. Bring to a boil.
4. Put the lamb into the crock-pot and pour tomato sauce over.
5. Cook for 8 hours on low.

Delicious Balsamic Lamb Chops:

Serves: 6

Preparation Time: 10 minutes

Cooking Time: 6 hours

Macros per serving:

Calories: 496

Protein: 72.7 grams

Fat: 19.1 grams

Carbohydrates: 1.8 grams

What you'll need:
- 3.4 lbs. lamb chops, trimmed off
- ½ teaspoon ground black pepper
- 2 tablespoons rosemary
- 2 tablespoons balsamic vinegar

- 4 garlic cloves, minced
- 1 large onion, sliced
- ½ teaspoon salt

How to make it:

1. Add onion into the bottom of slow cooker.
2. Place lamb chops on top of onions, then and rosemary, vinegar, garlic, pepper, and salt.
3. Cover and cook on low for 6 hours.
4. Serve and enjoy.

Pot Roast Soup:

Serves: 4

Preparation Time: 15 minutes

Cooking Time: 8 hours

Macros per serving:

Calories: 211

Protein: 21.63 grams

Fat: 11.29 grams

Carbohydrates: 5.21 grams

What you'll need:
- 1 ¼ pound of meat stew
- 1 onion, diced
- 1 head cauliflower, diced
- 1 can diced tomatoes
- 1 Portobello mushroom, diced
- ¾ cup chicken stock
- 1 teaspoon dried basil
- 1 teaspoon dried oregano
- Salt and pepper to taste

How to make it:
1. Add all ingredients in the Crockpot.
2. Close the lid and cook on low for 8 hours or high for 5 hours.

Lamb Curry:

Serves: 2

Preparation Time: 25 minutes

Cooking Time: 8 hours

Macros per serving:

Calories: 554

Protein: 28 grams

Fat: 42 grams

Carbohydrates: 4 grams

What you'll need:
- 1 lamb shoulder
- 1 tablespoon curry powder
- 1 tablespoon ground coriander powder
- ½ cup tomato paste

- 1 x 400ml can coconut cream

How to make it:

1. Place lamb shoulder, roughly diced onions, roughly chopped garlic and ¼ cup water in crock-pot.
2. Cover and cook on low for 6-8 hours.
3. Put the meat aside and add the onions and garlic from crock-pot to ma frying pan.
4. Add curry powder and coriander powder. Cook until they are integrated.
5. Add tomato paste and cooked lamb meat. Cook for a further 5 minutes
6. Add coconut cream and simmer for 10 minutes on low heat.

Crockpot Ropa Vieja:

Serves: 8

Preparation Time: 20 minutes

Cooking Time: 8 hours

Macros per serving:

Calories: 277

Protein: 37.13 grams

Fat: 12.14 grams

Carbohydrates: 3.01 grams

What you'll need:
- 2 tablespoons coconut oil
- 3 pounds flanks steak
- 2 cloves of garlic, minced
- 3 peppers, sliced
- ¼ cup parsley, chopped

- ¼ cup cilantro, chopped
- 1 cup water
- 1 tablespoon white wine vinegar
- 2 cans of tomato sauce
- 1 tablespoon onion powder
- 1 tablespoon cumin powder
- 1 tablespoon oregano
- Salt to taste

How to make it:

1. In a skillet, heat oil and sear the flank steak for 3 minutes on each side. Set aside.
2. Place garlic, peppers, parsley, and cilantro in the Crockpot.
3. Add in the seared flank steak.
4. Pour in water, vinegar, and tomato sauce.
5. Add in the onion powder, cumin, and oregano.
6. Season with salt to taste.
7. Close the lid and cook on low for eight hours.

Ground Lamb Casserole:

Serves: 2

Preparation Time: 5 minutes

Cooking Time: 8 hours

Macros per serving:

Calories: 295

Protein: 22 grams

Fat: 19 grams

Carbohydrates: 6 grams

What you'll need:
- 2 slices bacon, diced cooked crispy
- ½ lb. ground lamb
- 1/8 cup diced green bell pepper
- 2 cups thinly sliced cabbage

- 1 cup tomato sauce

How to make it:

1. Add the ground lamb, bacon, pepper, onion, and garlic to taste into the crock-pot.
2. Cover and cook for 6 hours in low.
3. Add the cabbage and tomato sauce to the pot, stir, then cook for another 2 hours.

Pork Recipes

Fabulous pork Casserole:

Serves: 8

Prep Time: 20minutes

Cook Time: 8hours 10 minutes

Macros per serving:

Calories: 296

Protein: 25.1grams

Fat: 17.6grams

Carbohydrates: 11grams

What you'll need:
- 1 tablespoon coconut oil

- 1 pound ground pork
- 1 onion, chopped
- 2 garlic cloves, minced
- ½ teaspoon red pepper flakes
- Salt, to taste
- 5 ounces fresh spinach
- 12 organic eggs
- 1 cup unsweetened coconut oil
- 1 pound butternut squash, peeled, seeded and chopped

How to make it:

1. Grease a crockpot
2. In a skillet, heat coconut oil and cook the pork for about 4-5 minutes
3. Stir in onion, garlic, red pepper flakes, and salt and cook for about 2-3 minutes.
4. Stir in spinach and cook for regarding a pair of minutes.
5. Remove from heat and keep aside to chill slightly.
6. To a bowl, add almond milk and eggs and beat well.
7. In the bottom of prepared crockpot, place squash, followed by pork mixture and egg mixture.
8. Set the crockpot on low and cook, covered, for about 6-8 hours.
9. Cut into 8 equal sized wedges and serve.

Chili Pulled Pork Tacos:

Serves: 10

Preparation Time: 10-15 minutes

Cooking Time: 8 hours

Macros per serving:

Calories: 159.8

Protein: 20.6 grams

Fat: 7 grams

Carbohydrates: 2.7 grams

What you'll need:
- 4 ½ pounds Pork meet butt or shoulder
- 1 ½ teaspoons Cumin grounded
- 2 tablespoons Chili powder
- ½ teaspoon Oregano grounded
- ½ cup Broth

- ¼ teaspoon Red pepper flakes
- 1 Bay leaf
- A pinch Grounded cloves
- Salt to taste

How to make it:

1. Combine salt, oregano, chili powder, cumin, cloves and pepper flakes in medium bowl.
2. Clean the pork and rub the spice mixture on the pork meet.
3. Keep it in the fridge for about 2 hours and let it get marinated properly.
4. Now keep ready your Crockpot slow cooker and put the marinated meet to it.
5. Add the broth and Bay leaf.
6. Cook it about 8 hours by setting on slow cooking.
7. Once cooking is over, place the cooked meet on a cutting board and by using two forks, and shred the meat.
8. Serve it hot.

Root Beer Pulled Pork:

Serves: 2

Preparation Time: 15 minutes

Cooking Time: 8 hours

Macros per serving:

Calories: 345

Protein: 18.6 grams

Fat: 27.8 grams

Carbohydrates: 4.3 grams

What you'll need:
- 1 (12 oz.)can or bottle root beer
- 1 (4 oz.) bottle liquid smoke flavoring, or to taste
- 1 (4 lb.)pork shoulder roast

How to make it:

1. Prepare the seasoning: salt, pepper, and garlic to taste.
2. Rub seasoning on all sides of pork.
3. Put the pork with all other ingredients in the Crockpot.
4. Cook for 8 hours on low.

Cuban Pulled Pork:

Serves: 6

Preparation Time: 10 minutes

Cooking Time: 8 hours

Macros per serving:

Calories: 461

Protein: 35.9 grams

Fat: 32.8 grams

Carbohydrates: 4.1 grams

What you'll need:

- 2 lbs. pork shoulder, cut into 4" pieces
- 2 tablespoons fresh cilantro, chopped
- ¼ teaspoon red pepper flakes
- 1 ½ teaspoons paprika
- 1 ½ teaspoons cumin
- 1 ½ teaspoon chili powder
- 1 tablespoon dry oregano
- ¼ cup oregano juice
- 3 garlic cloves, chopped
- 1 tablespoon lime juice
- 1 small onion, chopped
- ½ teaspoon salt

How to make it:

1. Add all ingredients into the slow cooker and stir well to mix.
2. Cover and cook on low for 8 hours.
3. Shred meat using a fork and serve.

Pork Stew with Oyster Mushrooms:

Serves: 4

Preparation Time: 15 minutes

Cooking Time: 6 hours

Macros per serving:

Calories: 374

Protein: 50.4 grams

Fat: 48.9 grams

Carbohydrates: 23.5 grams

What you'll need:
- 2 tablespoons coconut oil
- 1 onion, chopped
- 1 clove of garlic, chopped
- 2 pounds pork loin

- Salt and pepper to taste
- 2 tablespoons dried mustard
- 2 tablespoons dried oregano
- ½ teaspoon nutmeg powder
- 1 ½ cups bone broth
- 2 tablespoons white wine vinegar
- 2 pounds oyster mushroom
- ¼ cup coconut milk
- 3 tablespoons capers

How to make it:

1. Heat the Crockpot to high and add coconut oil.
2. Sauté the onion and garlic for two minutes and add in the pork loin. Sear and season with salt and pepper to taste.
3. Stir in the mustard, oregano, and nutmeg.
4. Pour in the bone broth and white wine vinegar
5. Add in the mushrooms.
6. Close the lid and adjust the cooking temperature to low.
7. Cook for 6 hours
8. Ten minutes before the cooking time, add in the coconut milk and capers.

Beamless Pork Chili:

Serves: 8

Preparation Time: 20 minutes

Cooking Time: 6 hours 10 minutes

Macros per serving:

Calories: 283

Protein: 20.4 grams

Fat: 17.3 grams

Carbohydrates: 9 grams

What you'll need:
- 2 medium green bell peppers, seeded and chopped
- 1 medium yellow onion, chopped
- ½ tablespoon olive oil
- 2 pounds lean ground pork

- Salt and freshly ground black pepper, to taste
- 8 thick bacon slices, chopped
- 2 cups tomatoes, chopped
- 1 ½ teaspoon ground cumin
- 2 teaspoons red chili powder
- ½ teaspoon cayenne pepper
- ¾ cup sugar-free tomato paste

How to make it:

1. In the bottom of a Crockpot, place bell pepper and onion.
2. In a large skillet, heat oil over medium-high heat and cook pork with salt and black pepper for about 4-5 minutes.
3. Transfer the pork into Crockpot.
4. In the same skillet, add bacon and cook for 4-5 minutes.
5. Place cooked bacon and tomatoes over pork and sprinkle evenly with spices.
6. Pour tomato paste on top evenly.
7. Set the Crockpot on low and cook, covered, for about 6 hours.

Pork Roast with Sugarless Chimichurri Sauce:

Serves: 12

Preparation Time: 30 minutes

Cooking Time: 6 hours

Macros per serving:

Calories: 167

Protein: 17 grams

Fat: 8 grams

Carbohydrates: 5 grams

What you'll need:
- 3 pounds Pork roast boneless
- 4 tablespoons Extra virgin olive oil

- 1 pound Carrots trimmed and quartered lengthwise
- Sweet onion thickly sliced
- Real salt to taste
- Chimichurri sauce (prepare as per the recipe)

How to make it:

1. Place the pork roasted in a pot. Add 2 tablespoons of the olive oil over the roast and sprinkle it with salt and pepper.
2. Cover and cook on high for 6 hours. In slow cooking, cook it about 12 hours.
3. After 4 hours of cooking, add the onions and carrots around the roast.
4. Cook the roast, carrots, and onions for 2 hours until you can easily pull apart the pork and the carrots become soft.
5. Place the roast, carrots, and onion on serving platter and drizzle with sauce.
6. Serve with extra sauce as per you like.

CONCLUSION

Thank you for reading this book and having the patience to try the recipes.

I do hope that you gain as much enjoyment reading and experimenting with the meals as I have had writing these books.

www.ingramcontent.com/pod-product-compliance
Lightning Source LLC
Chambersburg PA
CBHW071436070526
44578CB00001B/105